God's Girl

By

Rachel L. Johnson

Cameron —
May you alway
be God's girl!
Rachel L. Johnson

Published by Rachel L. Johnson
Sioux Falls, South Dakota

Printed by InstantPublisher.com

Table of Contents

Dedication

~~~~

This book is dedicated to my two princesses, Zoe and Gabrielle. It is my dearest prayer that you will follow the way of purity and be the women God designed you to be. I pray you see the value in the choices for purity that I made and make those same choices in your life.

May you always be God's girls! I love you both so much!

Mommy.

Preface

~~~~~

When I was in college and was asked to speak to teenagers on occasion, I got really nervous. I felt I did not have anything to say, because I did not have a testimony of reckless sin and forgiveness, so I wondered why they would want to hear from me. Most of the speakers I remembered from church camps and youth conventions had come out of a lifestyle of sin and were radically changed by the power of God. They had not grown up in the church and served the Lord their whole lives; so, in comparison, what I had to say would be boring and anti-climactic.

As I sought God about what to share with one particular youth group, the only message that came to me was "Stop being bad." It was all I could think of, but then the Lord spoke to me two things (I love it when He steps in and takes over. I needed it, too).

The first thing He told me was even though I had never committed any of the "big sins," as we tend to call them, I was still a sinner and lost without Him. It did not matter to God what level of sin I had committed against

Him; I was still a sinner in need of a Savior. It was the same blood that forgave my sins as forgave those with "big sins."

The second word the Lord spoke to my heart was that I *did* have a testimony -- I had a testimony every teenager could have. When I was 12 years old, I remember hearing Dr. James Dobson on the Focus on the Family radio program speak about the statistics of young people making a lot of bad choices before they reached the age of 20. I remember saying to myself, at that time, "I am going to make it to 20 years old without doing all those things." Shortly after I turned 20, I remember thinking, "I made it. I am 20, and I did not do all those things."

The Lord spoke to my heart that day and showed me that I could encourage young people to serve Him all the days of their lives and not have to do the things the world offers them. Through this time I spent with God, I was no longer nervous to share with teenagers but was excited to share my testimony with them. God had given me a testimony!

> I had a testimony every teenager could have.

Through examples and the Word of God, I want to encourage you to be God's girl all the days of your life. You do not have to be a statistic, and you can serve the Lord with all your heart and avoid the temptations the world is offering. This world is a tempting place, but in the midst, you can walk purely with God.

Through the power of the Holy Spirit you can walk through your teenage years with your head held high and your eyes fixed upon the Lord. The issue is not whether you will ever face temptation, but rather, when you are tempted, you have a way of escape. When you are in a tempting or trying situation, I hope you will say, "No, I will not, because I am God's girl." As you read ahead, this is going to become our motto so you can be reminded in times of temptation that God has already prepared a way out.

You are God's girl if you have chosen Him as your Lord and Savior. Each of you is special to God and you belong to Him. If you have not chosen to follow Him, you can at any time. Ask God to forgive you and wash away your sins. The Bible says in I John 1:9, "If we confess our sins He is faithful and just and will forgive us our sins and purify us from all unrighteousness."

You can accept salvation by: (A) Admitting you are a sinner and have done wrong, by telling God what you have done and that you are ready to turn from that sin. (B) Believe that Jesus is your Savior. You can ask Him into your heart and life. Pause right now and tell Jesus that you believe He is the Son of God and can forgive your sins. (C) Confess with your mouth that Jesus Christ is the Lord of your life. Tell someone that you have accepted Jesus into your heart and that you want to live for Him.

Introduction

~~~~~

For four years, my husband and I were youth pastors in northern California. Every year we held a purity retreat where we would challenge our students to walk in purity and holiness throughout their junior and senior high school years. Years after we left California, Andrea, one of our students, sent me a message, thanking me for what I had spoken at a purity retreat years before. It excited me that something I said years ago had impacted her life and had helped her stay pure and walking with the Lord.

This is the message I received from Andrea:

Hi Rachel,

I do not know if you remember me too much. I was in your youth group in Susanville. Anyway, the reason I'm writing this is to say thank you.

Right before I started my freshman year (ninth grade) of high school we had a purity youth retreat in the gym at SAG (Susanville Assembly of God) and I remember so vividly a few things that you said. I even remember what you were wearing: light blue jeans with pink flowers embroidered on them and a light pink shirt with red lipstick, that's how much it affected me...You stood in front of us and said, "Look at these lips, no cigarette, no alcohol, no drugs have ever touched these lips. You see this body, no vial thing has been done to it. It is pure. And you can have the same. You have God's strength to stand up to impurity in every form. You can do it."

I have never forgotten those words, and I never will. Because it gave me a hope that it is possible, and that I'm not the only one out there standing by those morals. And I'm standing strong, I've never compromised. And part of the strength that I found to stay pure 100 percent was through those words you spoke. So thank you.

Love Always,
Andrea

As I read that message over again, prompted by the Holy Spirit, I realized how many other precious young ladies need to hear the simple message that they can remain pure and walk with the Lord all the way through their teenage years. I decided to put my experience in writing to encourage as many young ladies as possible that they can remain pure, too.

My friend, let me encourage you, YOU CAN MAKE IT! You do not have to follow the ways of the world. You do not have to be another statistic; you can be God's girl. You need to be encouraged that others have gone before you and have walked pure even with the filth of the world all around them, and now it is your turn.

My prayer is that as you read this book you will be encouraged. I want you to be lifted in your spirit that you are God's girl and purity is possible. If Rachel and Andrea can make it, so can you! We welcome you to join us in this life of purity.

You are God's girl, and purity is possible!

Part 1
I Am God's Girl

Free To Be Me

~~~~

*"For you created my inmost being; you knit me together in my
mother's womb. I praise you because I am fearfully and wonderfully
made; your works are wonderful, I know that full well. My frame
was not hidden from you when I was made in the secret place.
When I was woven together in the depths of the earth, your eyes
saw my unformed body. All the days ordained for me were written
in your book before one of them came to be." Psalm 139:13*

I was born Rachel Lynne Meyers in August 1974.
Before I was born, my older sister, Aimee, was the first child
born to Robert and Renee Meyers of Fort Dodge, Iowa.
After me came my only brother, Rob, and then my little
sister, Robin, who does not like to be called my "little" sister
anymore now that she is over 30 years old, but she will always
be my "little sister."

This birth order arrangement became the key to who
I would become as it literally shaped who I was. My older
sister was special simply because she was the oldest. You
know how the oldest child is - they get their way, simply

because they were born first. It is not fair. My brother was also special, because he was the only boy and was definitely a mama's boy. My mother spent many hours holding his hand as he daydreamed about flying through space instead of doing his homework. At the end of the chain was my little sister who naturally was special since she was the baby. We even called her "Baby Bin" most of our growing up years together. That left me. There was nothing special about me; I was just there. My theme song growing up was "Nobody likes me; everybody hates me; guess I'll go eat worms." That was not a joke to me but really how I felt. I had no amazing qualities as I lived under the shadow of my older sister, always trying to be good at something, because she was good at everything.

We were poor farm kids growing up on a small farm in Shelby, Iowa. My clothes were hand-me-downs from my older sister, which were handed down to her from someone else. My hair was another issue. My mom was ill from complications of the birth of my younger sister and unable to do my hair or teach me how to do it. I remember I had a permed mullet I never liked. I remember trying to grow out my bangs to have long one-length hair, but then it hung in my eyes, and we would cut it all over again. I just wanted to be pretty but never could gain that confidence. To complicate the matter, my dad bought us cowboy boots and made us wear them to school. They made loud clomping sounds on the hardwood floors no matter how softly I walked, and I remember the kids would stare and laugh at me. To induce further humiliation we had to wear bulky snowsuits and snow boots in the winter instead of cute winter coats and stylish boots.

Despite living in Iowa, we went to church at Glad Tidings in Omaha, Nebraska, about 40 miles away. The people in that church were very well-off compared to us. I remember feeling like we were the country bumpkins going to the city church. I would not have known where to buy the "fancy" name-brand clothes the other girls wore even if my parents would have had the money. My clothes were worlds apart from the clothes they wore.

Learning ways to minister in the church came early for me. My dad is very musical, and when we were elementary- age, he would play the piano and have Mom, my siblings and me sing. On occasion, he would take us to very small Pentecostal churches, especially on Sunday nights to have our family sing. We grew up singing and ministering in these various churches, and I learned early to be adaptable to different ministry settings. To this day, we have an old video of my sister Aimee and I singing at a small Christian television station when we were 4 and 5 years old. Through singing even in small audiences, I learned to be in front of people, and I learned I loved ministering for the Lord. In spite of what other people thought of me on the outside, and how I viewed myself, God was working on me at an early age. He was molding and shaping my heart for Him, though I was not much to look at on the outside and felt insignificant.

Growing up on the farm, there were times when I would talk to the Lord while feeding the animals or walking out in the cornfield. Thankfully, His presence goes with us wherever we are, and He did not care I was with the animals or working in the garden -- He was still there speaking to me. David in the Bible was a shepherd boy and in the midst of his caring for the sheep he wrote songs unto the Lord. He even fought off wild animals while tending his sheep, but David had no idea God was preparing him to be the leader of a great army, and later a great nation, while he did what seemed insignificant: out in a field watching sheep. You never know where small beginnings will take you.

Zechariah 4:10 says, "Who despises the day of small things?"

I did not know God was preparing me to minister for Him while I was enjoying His presence on the farm. I just knew I loved the Lord and loved being with Him whenever and wherever I could, but my appearance still affected me.

I went to high school in the late 80s-early 90s when big hair was in, and I had the biggest of them all. I inhaled gallons of hairspray trying to get my hair just right. I wore tons of make-up and clothes that I thought would make me look nice. I wanted to be pretty like the rich girls but did not know how. No one had taught me how to dress properly, put on make-up or do my hair. The experience was trial and error, but mainly ended up in error. If it was not for Aimee telling me my hair was too big, I may have taken the door frames off a few doors; it was that high!

We all get a good laugh when we look back at the way people used to dress. If you came to my house and saw old pictures of me through the years, we would laugh until our sides ached. But, in honesty, I was trying to look nice but did not know until later how silly I really looked. I guess that is the price-tag for taking fashion to the extreme.

1 Samuel 16:7 says, "The LORD does not look at the things man looks at. Man looks at the outward appearance, but the LORD looks at the heart."

I am grateful that despite my lack of fashion and beauty sense, God still had His hand on my life. At least the Lord knew He could work on my hair as long as He had my heart first!

With my childhood church, I had the opportunity to attend kid's camps, retreats, youth camps, youth conventions and many other special events. The problem was, for me, my clothes were very unstylish and not cool enough for the other girls who also attended. No one wanted to borrow my clothes, and some of them actually did not want to even room with me at all. It really hurt my self-esteem and still even hurts to remember now. I felt I was never good enough. I was always looked down on as the dirty, little farm girl.

Since, many of us went onto college and got married, and I have not seen many of those girls since high school. But now, Facebook has brought us back into contact again. When I "friend" some of the girls that I knew from my church youth group, I see nice homes, picture-perfect families, lovely husbands and prosperous lives. At first, I felt the same as I had years ago, and saw myself as the little girl that they had avoided and looked down upon. But seeing them now as adults and talking with them online, I see lives that are not so perfect. Their beautiful clothes are covering up messy lives and their hearts turned away from God.

It hurts to see these women following the patterns of this world. I ask myself, "Didn't we all attend the same church? Didn't we all attend the same youth conventions? What caused me to follow Christ and others to turn away?" It grieves my heart that Satan has deceived so many.

As you go through junior high, high school, college, and on throughout your life, do not be fooled, girls, when you look around you and see people's lives that you envy, because it seems they have it all together. I assure you, it is simply not so. The devil himself will ensure every life has trouble, yours and mine included. The truth, however, is we are all women made by God. You may not be the prettiest girl in your class. You may not be the tallest or the skinniest, but as the Word of God says in Psalm 139:14, "You are fearfully and wonderfully made." God made you exactly like He wanted you to be.

There are so many different types of people in the world. You cannot be all of them.

I have seen thousands of people in my lifetime, at work, the mall, fairs, church, etc. I have learned a few things through my 30-plus years I feel will help you.

I will never be the skinniest person in the world.

I will never be the heaviest person in the world.

I will never be the shortest person in the world.

I will never be the tallest person in the world.

22

I will never be the ugliest person in the world.

I will never be the prettiest person in the world.

I will never be the most tan person in world.

I will never be the palest person in the world.

I will never have the longest hair in the world.

I will never have the shortest hair in the world.

I will never dress the nicest in the world.

I will never dress the worst in the world.

I will never have brownest eyes in the world....

I think you get the picture. There are so many different types of people in the world. You cannot be all of them. God is creative, and He enjoys making all shapes, sizes and colors of people. You will go crazy trying to be anyone else but you. Take who YOU are and make it the best from the inside out. Let your heart be shaped first. God has a plan for your life to use you if you will let Him. You were special to God before you were even born.

Jeremiah 1:5 says, "Before I formed you in the womb, I knew you, before you were born I set you apart; I appointed you as a prophet to the nations."

As a child and teenager, I may not have been much to look at on the outside, but on the inside, God was molding my heart. During years spent in Bible quiz, we hid the Word of God in our hearts. In Missionettes, a church sponsored girl's club, we memorized Scripture and did projects to shape us into being God's girls. In our fine arts competition, we learned to use our talents for God, no matter if we were very good or not.

I know some teenagers from my church who won the fine arts competition at the national level, but today never use the talents they were given. I did not even win my church level, but I continued to improve and never gave up pursuing what God had put in my heart. I wanted to give up many times, because I was not very talented, but instead I improved on the little talent I had. In life, it truly is not about who starts but who finishes. It is not even about who has the most talent but who is willing to develop even the smallest talent they do have.

I am grateful God did not reject me because I was unlovely to look at. He was shaping my heart and planting His Word deep into good soil so seeds could grow and bear fruit. God is able to take our inadequacies and insecurities and use us anyway. He is always looking for willing vessels; not the prettiest, skinniest, most talented vessels!

Discussion Questions

1. What insecurities do you struggle with in your life?
2. What are the areas in your heart God needs to work on? Are you willing to submit those to Him?
3. Read again Psalm 139:13 at the beginning of the chapter. What does that scripture mean to you?

Growing But Not There Yet

~~~~~

"These things happened to them as examples and were written down as warnings for us." I Corinthians 10:6

After graduating from high school in 1992, I went to North Central Bible College in Minneapolis, Minnesota. I was naïve and innocent when I went. Being a Christian college, I thought everyone there would be in love with Jesus and want to serve Him with all their heart. I thought all the guys would be radical and holy, but it did not take long for me to figure out this was not the case. Many were not different from guys I went to high school with, except they were supposed to be Christians.

At one point in my freshman year, I was asked to go on a walk with a guy. I agreed, but during the walk when we stopped to look over a bridge, he started to kiss me. I was angry, because I did not know him or even like him, yet here he was trying to kiss me! It was awkward, and I was grossed out. It made me mad to think he could kiss some random girl he had recently met and barely knew. Ashamed of his actions, I quickly ended the walk and never talked to him again! I was given a choice, give in or stand up for my convictions.

The following summer, another guy I knew casually crossed my path as I was walking across the street on campus. He asked me what I was doing, I said, "Nothing," and then he invited me to his apartment to hang out with him and his roommate. Again, being innocent and trusting, I agreed. Not long after we got there his roommate left, and we were alone. At the time, I did not really think anything of it, because I was at Bible college, until I realized he was not there to chat and hang out. He, too, came close to me and tried to kiss me (I still do not know why some guys think it is OK to kiss random girls; I thought kissing was something special shared by two people in love). I once again took my cue, made up an excuse and left as fast as I could. I was not going to be swept off my feet by some guy I knew did not even like me. On a sad note, a year later he left college, because he got a young girl pregnant during his pastoral internship.

I want to pause here for a moment for a very important note to young girls. When a guy asks you to his apartment, room, car, etc., he probably is not looking to hang out and chat like girls do when they get together. There is a reason rape happens at the rate it does on college campuses. Take my warning and never ever be alone with a guy. I was glad God was watching over me, because this story may have had a very different ending.

I Corinthians 10:1-13

For I do not want you to be ignorant
of the fact, brothers, that our
forefathers were all under the cloud

and that they all passed through the sea. They were all baptized into Moses in the cloud and in the sea. They all ate the same spiritual food and drank the same spiritual drink; for they drank from the spiritual rock that accompanied them, and that rock was Christ. Nevertheless, God was not pleased with most of them; their bodies were scattered over the desert. Now these things occurred as examples to keep us from setting our hearts on evil things as they did. Do not be idolaters, as some of them were; as it is written: "The people sat down to eat and drink and got up to indulge in pagan revelry." We should not commit sexual immorality, as some of them did — and in one day twenty-three thousand of them died. We should not test the Lord, as some of them did — and were killed by snakes. And do not grumble, as some of them did — and were killed by the destroying angel. These things happened to them as examples and were written down as warnings for us, on whom the fulfillment of the ages has come. So, if you think you are standing firm, be careful that you don't fall! No temptation has seized you except what is common to man.

And God is faithful; he will not let
you be tempted beyond what you can
bear. But when you are tempted, he
will also provide a way out so that you
can stand up under it.

Paul the Apostle wrote this chapter to the Corinthians
as a warning. Verses one through five show how God
performed all kinds of miracles for the children of Israel
while in the wilderness close to His presence. Yet even with
all the miracles and the presence of God Himself, they still
sinned! I always wondered how that could happen, until I
realized, I am just like them. Take church camp as an
example. God shows up at camp, and we know He is real,
and we see Him moving at the altars, but oddly the next day
we treat our parents with disrespect when they come to pick
us up. Maybe we are not so different from the Israelites.

In verse six, Paul says the Corinthians experienced all
these things as examples to you and me. They were written
down for us in God's word as warnings for us. The Word of
God was not just recorded so we know what the Israelites
were like, but the stories were written to teach us. If the
stories of the Bible were meant for us, then let us take the
warning and heed it. Let us not be those who act one way
when God's presence is around and another way around our
unsaved friends. We should strive to be consistent in our
walk with the Lord.

In verse 12 of this segment of scripture, Paul says that
we are to be careful if we think we are standing firm and
everything is all right. Just because things are going OK now
does not mean it will still be that way in a few minutes. Be
alert; be watching for those traps, as the devil is trying to lay
out stumbling blocks for you. He desires nothing less than

for you to stumble, fall, and never get up to be God's girl again.

Finally, in verse 13, Paul says to us these famous words, "Temptation is common to all men." We are all tempted. I am tempted, and you are tempted. The good news is God will give you the strength to overcome the temptation if you depend on Him. In every area of your life where you face temptation, God has already provided a way out! You do not need to worry. If you decide purity is the way you want to live your life, then God is on your side. He will go ahead of you and will protect you so that nothing will overtake you. God's girl, that is encouraging news! You can be pure, knowing you are not the first girl to face temptation and you will not be the last. You have permission to say "No" because you belong to Him!

Every day we need to be listening to our parents, youth leaders, and those God has placed around us for guidance. You are growing up, but you are not there yet. Be wise and remember there is value in listening to those who have gone ahead. There are many lessons still to be learned, and the more you open yourself to learn them, the less they might hurt.

It may seem like everyone is out to get you and tell you that you cannot have any fun, but that is not true at all. Christians can have a lot of fun and avoid waking up the next morning and regretting it. If the Lord asks us to sacrifice something, there is a greater reward up ahead.

I have two daughters that are home-schooled, and one of the common topics spoken about at the parenting conferences is instilling character within your children. In our home we do that by example. There are many illustrations of people's lives in the Bible, classical literature and modern-day stories where valuable lessons from the mistakes or good choices of others are taught. Even at my age I would be wrong to stop learning and studying the lives of people.

One conference speaker my husband and I like is Mark Hamby. Through his teachings, he has helped us raise our children. I, particularly, tend to be very strict and structured with the girls, but Mark has helped me to show my girls mercy and balance out the style of parenting I am most comfortable with. I cannot say, "I have been a mom for eight years now, so I've got it all together and know how to do this thing." That would be crazy. Even as my girls grow into teenagers, I plan to read books from other moms who have experienced both the good and the bad in raising teenage girls. I cannot pretend I am the only mom in the world who knows what she is doing when I have not been to that stage in my life yet.

The similar truth goes for you. It would be an understatement that you have arrived and know everything there is to being a teenager and how to be pure. Take it from me; your teenage years will be a lot easier if you study books by those who have made mistakes as a teenager and from those who chose to walk in purity. Learn from others. We can all be students in whatever stage of life we are in, but it is important to understand we will never "arrive" until the day we die and go to Heaven. Until that day we see Jesus, we are in need of each other and the lessons that we can learn along the way.

As God's girls, we should desire to learn from those around us. If someone warns you that putting your hand in a fire will hurt, you are grateful they warned you. If someone tells you to remain pure, you should be grateful to them as well. Do you tend to listen to the leadership God has placed in your life, or is it easy to blow them off?

Matthew 24:35 says, "Heaven and earth will pass away but my words will never pass away."

The Word of God is eternal. It was spoken into existence thousands of years ago and will last forever. Trust me; it is not just suggestions for old-fashioned living. In honesty, it has tools for everyone, in every culture, everywhere. Biblical values may seem old-fashioned, but they are also futuristic at the same time. No matter what era of time we live in, God's word remains relevant and is our rule book to follow.

We need to decide if we are going to follow the Bible and its principles, even when it hurts. What if following a life of purity cost you your friendships? Would you do it then? What if you are made fun of? What if you are no longer popular? Is being God's girl worth everything to you?

Discussion Questions

1. Can you think of an example of a time you were warned not to do something and you did it anyway? What was the outcome?
2. Is there someone in your life who deserves more respect for the things they are trying to teach you?
3. Are you teachable? If not, how can you be more willing to learn?

The Gift Of Purity

~~~~

"Blessed are the pure in heart for they will see God." Matthew 5:8

What is purity? Is it a line that we can step over and then suddenly become impure? How do we know if we are pure? I like to view purity as a gift, a present that you are given at birth. Purity is a beautiful, white, spotless gift you are to carry with you and give to your husband on your wedding night.

As little girls, we are not aware that we have this gift, but as we grow into teenagers we realize we have a gift. We slowly become aware of the gift God has given us. As we have already discussed, the gifts come in all different colors, shapes and sizes. There are no two gifts alike. Each is unique and individual. There is only one of you. You are a unique gift! Cherish the uniqueness of you!

At the same time girls are becoming aware of their gift, boys are also becoming aware of these lovely gifts, too. The boys begin to do what I call "gift shopping." The boys begin to notice girls in a different way than they have before. The girls they beat up on in elementary school they now see as gifts to be chosen.

One mistake girls make during this time is we like to take our gift and begin to show it off to the boys. Maybe we flirt a little or tease them. We may even dress differently in order to get the "shopper's" attention. We do not want to be the gift that remains on the shelf; we want to be chosen, but sometimes we go about it the wrong way. A true man of God is looking for a gift that is pure in every way and degrading yourself for the sake of attention is not wholesome.

> Purity is a gift you are given at birth to carry with you to your wedding night.

One way to help the guys who are striving themselves to be pure is to see them as your brother. The guys who are Christians and are walking the same path with us need our help. When you see the guys around you as your brother, it is a lot easier to dress properly. It is easier to not flirt and play with their emotions, and for sure, you would not hold hands, kiss or make-out with your brother. Guys deserve our help in their walk of purity as well.

There are many different types of male shoppers out there, and some guys just want to look at all the gifts because they are gorgeous. Other guys begin to touch the gifts, because it is hard to resist. Still some may try to unwrap the gift to see how much they can gain for their prize. For others, they think opening the gift is alright, because ultimately, they believe, it can be wrapped back up again. But if you are anything like me, you know opening gifts before Christmas ruins the fun of Christmas morning and you never quite get it wrapped again like mama had it.

This is where we can ask ourselves how much of the gift am I willing to keep for my wedding night? Holding hands? Hugging? Kissing? Making out? Sex? How much are you willing to keep for that one man God has for you, or are you OK with wrapping the gift back up? Will your future husband be OK when you tell him how many guys you have allowed to use this gift before him?

Inevitably, before you get married one day, you will have to sit down and have a talk with your fiancé. You will either dread telling him about your past or proudly tell him you saved your gift for him. Imagine the look on this wonderful man's face when he has to deal with the fact that you already opened the gift meant for him. Or, on the other hand, imagine the joy you will share knowing you have a gift that you have saved and cannot wait to give him.

God designed sex to be a beautiful, holy and delightful gift shared between two married people. How delightful it will be for you and your husband to open up this gift together on your wedding night without prior use and baggage attached to it. It will be fun and guilt-free to open up the gift you have saved for him. There will be no bad memories of all the others who used the gift in the past. I pray you will want to cherish this gift and give it unopened and unused to a very special man God has been preparing for you.

If you can, pause and read the book of the Song of Solomon in the Bible. When I read the Song of Solomon I want the love that Solomon and his wife have to be the same experience for you. What a precious book of the Bible as these love birds flitter and flutter about, telling of their greatest desires for each other. They run through various hills and fields looking for each other. They call to one another through the windows to come and be together. She declares throughout Israel how handsome, charming and magnificent he is. She does not have enough words to describe this amazing man she has found. Then King Solomon answers with the funniest descriptions of her beauty. He says in chapter four:

> How beautiful you are, my darling!
> Oh, how beautiful!
> Your eyes behind your veil are doves.
> Your hair is like a flock of goats
> descending from Mount Gilead.

> Your teeth are like a flock of sheep just shorn,
> coming up from the washing.
> Each has its twin;
> not one of them is alone.

> Your lips are like a scarlet ribbon;
> your mouth is lovely.
> Your temples behind your veil
> are like the halves of a pomegranate.

> Your neck is like the tower of David,
> built with elegance;
> on it hang a thousand shields,
> all of them shields of warriors.

We would never use these metaphors today, but you can feel the love that he has for her. It is overwhelming the emotion that this book has. We long for the connection Solomon and his lover have, and God's plan is for each of us to experience true love; that is why the Song of Solomon is in the Bible. God is showing us the love He has for us, but also the true love that a man and wife can have when they follow God's plan. When we are willing to cherish the gift of purity God has given us, there is great joy in opening the gift.

Discussion Questions

1. How can we cherish the gift we have been given?
2. How can we truly experience the love of Solomon and his wife?
3. How does seeing the guys around you as your brothers help you?

Part 2
Protecting God's Girl

The Dating Debate

~~~~~

"Above all else, guard your heart, for it is the wellspring of life."
Psalm 4:23

As I have mentioned before, when my husband, Jeremiah, and I were youth pastors, we held a dating series during Wednesday night services or a purity retreat each year. One of the aspects of the services and retreats was to have a live debate with one group of students arguing for dating and another group of students arguing against dating. The first year everyone wanted to be on the side of debating for dating, but as the years went on, everyone wanted to be on the other team. Everyone knew the "pro-dating team" would have a hard time coming up with material. I would tease them to come up with a good reason for dating, but none of them could. Recently, I put a post on my Facebook page for someone to give me one good reason to date in high school. To my surprise, in reply, most people told me they wish they had not dated.

Is there one good reason to date someone in high school instead of simply being their friend? What are the benefits of dating you cannot get from being friends? Do you know the answer? The answer is really nothing outside of the physical. The only "benefit" to dating instead of being friends and actually getting to know one another is the physical aspect of a relationship. Everything else you can get by being friends and keeping it pure.

When you are friends, you enjoy spending time together, talking, hanging out, texting or posting pictures of each other on Facebook. As you do that, you continually get to know one another in a healthy way. There is no pressure; you enjoy bumping into them in the hall at school and are glad when they want to do something with you. But, if one of you wants to walk away and no longer be friends, no harm is done. Maybe you stop hanging out, texting all night and chatting online. Sometimes, you do not even purposely stop being friends; it just happens when one of you finds another friend with more in common or you get too busy to be together as much. Later you may miss parts of the friendship, but sometimes you do not even realize you are not close friends anymore.

I had a friend names "Matt," when I was in high school. Our parents were friends, and we attended the same church. He was in the youth group, and we had a fun time whenever we could be together. He really liked me, and the other kids in the youth group would ask me if I wanted go out with him. I never wanted to go out with him, but yet, I would go to his house to hang out, and we would do a lot of stuff together. We would sit by each other in church and youth group. I looked forward to seeing him on Sundays and Wednesday nights, and we even made up excuses to get together, but I really just liked being his friend. I did have strong feelings for him, but we never dated simply because I did not want to. To this very day, our families stay in contact. I love his parents, because they are sweet people of God; they even came to my wedding. I often wonder if things would be the same today if I had dated him and we had to break up. He has a family of his own now, and I would love to chat with him sometime and meet his wife and kids. It would not be awkward at all, because we were never anything more than friends who slowly drifted apart through changes in life. We never had to break up.

The opposite of friendship is dating.

The best benefit of having friends of the opposite sex is you can have lots of other friends at the same time and neither is threatened by the other friends. You are a group of friends who enjoy doing the same things, have the same goals, live in the same area or go to the same youth group. You are all friends.

I see the opposite of friendship being dating. You ask, "How can that be?" In a dating relationship, there is constant pressure. Once you say "We are dating," or "We are going out," the only way out is to break up. If you are dating someone in the ninth grade, what are your chances of getting married? The odds of actually making it to the altar are minimal and even after four years, friendship would be a lot less stressful. We hear of high school sweethearts, but really, there are more break-ups than knots tied.

So why do teenagers date? I would say one reason is so they can belong to someone. Many young ladies do not have fathers that are in their homes, and they need support from someone. Even if that someone is not perfect, at least he is there. How many young ladies date guys they kind of like just because he will care for her and give her emotional support? This is where girls can get into trouble with dating guys that may offer them drugs, alcohol or sex, and they accept it, because he is their emotional support.

Some girls will date guys just to get kissed so they can say they have kissed a guy. Girls, please do not buy that line. You are no less valuable because you have never been kissed. Are you really more valuable because you have kissed a boy? No, you are valuable just being you.

The pressure is on to perform when you are dating. "Does he still like me today?" "Did he change his mind overnight?" "Did he find someone else he likes better?" "He did not text me good night so I cannot go to sleep. He must not like me anymore." "I think he just looked at another girl." "Why does he have her phone number?" The list is endless. In a friendship, this may be overlooked. Girls, our emotions can be like a yo-yo when we date someone. We may feel in love one minute, and rejected the next because of his actions, potentially causing emotional instability.

The largest reason young people feel the need to date is they desire physical touch. Some even crave it. Many girls might not get love from their fathers, who may not be in the home or more likely living in another home with their step-mom, and as a result, hormone-filled teenage boys have lended to that need. If that is you, this does not need to be your story. Why replace Daddy's love with lust from a teenage boy? Psalm 68:5 says that God Himself will be a "Father to the fatherless." He will be there for you when you need to be loved. He will not use you and dump you, nor will He ever break up with you. If you recognize this is you, ask God to fill that void for you.

Psalm 18:24 says, "He is a friend that sticks closer than a brother."

Girls, there is a problem once you give in to the physical aspect of a relationship. The Bible says in Proverbs 4:23, "Above all else, guard your heart, for it is the wellspring of life." But girls, we do not guard our hearts! We put them out on display just hoping Prince Charming will come along and take it. "Here's my heart, break it," is what we are conveying. Once you start small physical gestures like holding hands, then you have to keep going further and further. When holding hands no longer satisfies, you have to do more - from the hands it moves to your arms around each other, and on and on. Finally, you get to the point in your relationship, if you allow physical touch to progress, that there is nothing left but sex. You break up, and the cycle starts all over when you start dating the next guy, except this time you are aware what is down the road so the "holding hands" time frame is shorter and the physical progresses a lot faster this time.

Where do you draw the line? Like we talked about in the last chapter, you need to decide how much of the gift you want opened and how much you want to save for your husband. When you date guy after guy it gets harder to keep that gift untouched for later.

At some point, the inevitable happens and you break up. The result is heartache, loss of appetite, decluttering his stuff from your room and changing your relationship status on Facebook. It can be a mess. Sooner or later your friends are even divided, because some are his friends and some are yours. Can anyone really "just be friends" after a break-up? Not usually, as you avoid each other at school, walk different ways to classes, and you may not even go to your youth group anymore. As a result, your whole life can suffer an adult-sized emotional trauma. Everything seems to be a mess, because you wrapped all your emotions and identity into being a couple. Is dating the opposite of friendship? Once the dating is over, the friendship is gone, too. I have never broke up with one of my friends before -- I have chosen not to hang out with them anymore -- but there was not a traumatic ending.

Girls, I have been there. I know it is hard when he is cute, he likes you and he wants to take you out. Instead of going on a date, why not hang out with a group in a safe public place? Perhaps his perfection will wear off, then at least you hung out where you could get to know the real him. It is OK to do all kinds of things together as friends. That is what I did with several guys in high school. Then when I realized there were certain things I did not like about them, no harm was done.

When I first began getting to know Jeremiah, he was a senior in high school and I was his youth pastor. Because we knew there was going to be no dating until he graduated and went to college, we spent many hours at his grandparents' home. We would eat dinner there and watch country music television, because that is what his grandparents liked -- or basketball, because that is what he liked. I was a regular guest in their home at their request. It was safe there, and it allowed me to get to know the real Jeremiah, because I got to know his family. I saw how he treated his grandparents and saw how he interacted with his family. I got to know the personalities of his family members, and even today I can see how that made him who he is.

Even though a small town, like the one we lived in, can be boring, we found things to do. We took walks, learned to run, rented movies, went places with his family, and of course, there were the endless church events that we did together.

During this time I lived with a girl, Shannon, and the three of us would do a lot of things together. We were all good friends, and I loved Shannon to pieces. It was great to have someone to talk things over with and be there for accountability. She was a wise counselor and had great insight into relationships. The bond the three of us shared is still alive today. The three of us ministered together at different churches, youth groups, jails and missions -- we would sing, perform dramas and preach. But we would have fun and goof off together, too. Shannon became my best friend and Jeremiah became my husband. It was a win-win situation.

Girls, I know I probably will not win popularity by writing these things in this chapter, and it may seem impossible for young people of your generation to grasp, but

I'm trying to save you a lot of heartache and emotional trauma. You are worth it!

Many of you may say we are "just friends" or that you just have a crush on a particular guy, but you hold the guy in your heart as your own. You are jealous when someone else talks to him; you expect him to talk to you and are depressed when he does not. You call and text all hours of the day; your emotions ride a roller coaster all day long based on his actions. There is an unhealthy emotional bond there that you have allowed to grow when you base your entire day on him, and it is going to destroy you. You need to release those emotional ties and let him go while you enjoy your teenage years. He does not belong to you. Do not form emotional ties that keep you dependent on a guy for your happiness.

Discussion Questions

1. What benefits can you think of that dating has over friendship?
2. What benefits can you see that friendship has over dating?
3. Are you willing to go against the flow of what is popular in order to save yourself a lot of heartache?

Your Sins Will Find You Out

~~~~~

"He chose to be mistreated along with the people of God rather than to enjoy the pleasures of sin for a short time." Hebrews 11:25

Moses was an amazing man. Hebrews 11:25 refers to a time in his life as a young man when he had all the pleasures of Egypt at his fingertips, because he was the adopted son of the princess. He could have had anything he wanted, but instead of lavishing himself in those pleasures he chose to follow God and suffer with the children of Israel, his true family. He understood the things Egypt had to offer him were only temporary; he knew they would not last and he would be left empty.

Today we do not always see things that way. Society tells us we have a right to feel good and constantly be comfortable. If anything disturbs us, we eat ice cream to soothe our pain (or at least I do). Girls, serving God and following the Bible is not always going to be comfortable. It may hurt sometimes to say no.

The mainstream media paints a portrait of relationships being incredibly casual. Many people in the spotlight show us you do not even have to be boyfriend and girlfriend to make out and ultimately sleep together. The world portrays this all the time on television shows as two people sleep together like it was an accident. Have you heard your friends say, "It just happened," like they could not do anything about it? Some shows go as far as to say, "That was a good time, what is your name?" The world may think this casual relationship is humor, but God does not. In the Old Testament, sex outside of marriage would lead to death if caught.

Through the few stories I have already shared, you can see there were many guys out there who were willing to fool around with me without even thinking twice. Some of those boys get what they want physically but might not even remember who you are the next day. Many teenage boys have little control of the raging hormones within them, and as godly young ladies we have to be in the driver's seat. We need to be strong enough to say, "No, thank you."

A friend of mine, evangelist Dean Niforatos, said, "You can choose your sins, but you can't choose your consequences." If you choose to go against God's laws as Hebrews 11:25 says, "It will be pleasurable for a short time," but there will be a price to pay in the end. What price is there to pay? Let's look at some of the possible consequences of those who choose to have sex before marriage.

1. Sexually transmitted diseases (STDs)

Reality has it that if he is sleeping with you, he probably has already slept with someone else. Multiple sex partners increases the likelihood and the probability of contracting an STD. The more guys you sleep with, the higher probability you have in contracting an STD.

There are more than 50 strains of STDs. Not all of them can be cured, and only some can only be maintained. Gonorrhea, chlamydia, syphilis, genital herpes, genital warts, HIV/AIDS, hepatitis and crabs are the most common. HIV/AIDS, hepatitis, herpes and genital warts are never cured; they are only managed. Worse, you will become able to pass this nasty germ along to your next partner, sometimes without even knowing you are infected. HIV/AIDS and hepatitis are passed through the body and become bloodborne pathogens; these are manageable but not treatable. (1)

A few other facts about STDs:

•Of the 18.9 million new cases of STDs each year, 9.1 million, occur among 15 through 24-year-olds. (2)

•Although 15 through 24-year-olds represent only one-quarter of the sexually active population, they account for nearly half of all new STDs each year. (2)

•Human papillomavirus (HPV) infections account for about half of STDs diagnosed among 15 through 24-year-olds each year. HPV is extremely common, often asymptomatic and generally harmless. However, certain types,

51

if left undetected and untreated can lead to cervical cancer. (2)

2. Cervical cancer

Cervical cancer is a sexually transmitted disease directly linked to sleeping with multiple partners. A friend, Dr. Addison Tolentino, says that the more people you sleep with, the more your risk for cervical cancer increases. When the world is promoting sex before marriage, they do not know that they are putting themselves at risk for a deadly disease. God knew what He was talking about when He said to be pure before you get married and remain faithful when you do get married!

3. Pregnancy

My children cannot imagine how anyone could not love a baby. They tell me how cute babies are and how much they love taking care of them. Yes, they are cute, but little do they understand the real work in caring for a newborn baby. Caring for a baby is very difficult for a full-time adult mom who wanted a baby, and it is even harder work for a teenager who had an unplanned pregnancy because of finances, balancing her own education and unknown support from the child's father.

The United States has the highest teen pregnancy rate in the industrialized world. According to the Center for Disease control, one-third of teenage girls get pregnant before the age of 20. Teenpregnancy.org states, "750,000 teen pregnancies occur annually. Eight in 10 of these pregnancies are unintended and 81 percent are to unmarried teens." (3)

I must say, if there was one thing in my life that changed me more than anything else, it was having a baby. Getting married was easy compared to caring for a baby 24 hours a day. I was 28 years old when I had Zoe, and I had no idea how to care for a newborn. The experience literally rocked my world, and I can say I have never been the same to this day. Sadly, there are thousands of teen girls having babies, leaving school and never fulfilling the dreams in their heart. As a result we have a phenomenon of "babies raising babies."

As the saying goes, "If you play with fire, you will get burned." You do not have to worry about having a baby if you stay pure until marriage.

One of the greatest blessings that can come from a teenage pregnancy is adoption. Hundreds of married couples cannot have babies but are emotionally and financially capable to adopt and willing to do so if they are given the opportunity. One loving option for unwed mothers to make for their baby is to allow a loving Christian couple to raise and train the child in godliness. There is a lot of information, help and support available on adoption.

> Getting married was easy compared to having a baby.

53

The largest Christian adoption agency is Bethany Christian Services. Bethany provides adoption services and care for women with unplanned pregnancies. They, and others like them, give counsel and hope to young girls all over the United States. If you or a friend is in this situation, please consider contacting Bethany Christian Services at Bethany.org.

4. Abortion

I can hardly think about abortion without feeling sick. I cannot imagine in such an advanced society, with the ultrasound technology available, that anyone could actually deny what is growing inside a woman's body is a baby. I believe you would have to literally turn a blind eye and a deaf ear to believe the lie that it is just a blob of tissue, a non-human until it breathes. Abortion doctors even tell girls that their baby has no feelings. I wonder, according to the doctors, when they get feelings? Is it as they are coming down the birth canal? Videos taken of abortions show the screams of little tiny babies and the distortion on their faces showing just how much it hurts to be burned to death or pulled apart limb by limb.

Having a baby at 29 weeks gestation, about six and a half months along, I have a different view on abortion than most. Our second daughter, Gabrielle, was born two and a half months early. Before she was born, even at 29 weeks, I could have aborted her in some states (A normal pregnancy is about 40 weeks). The thought makes me sad. When Gabrielle was born she was a perfect little baby, but extremely small. She had 10 toes, 10 fingers, and tiny legs, arms and hands; she could cry and she had dirty diapers. There was nothing different about Gabrielle physically other than some internal parts of her were immature. Her lungs were developed, but just not mature enough take in enough oxygen on their own. Every part of her was a human -- she was not a blob -- she was a human even though she was not supposed to be born yet. She was a very tiny, 100 percent human baby. She cried as the nurses poked needles into her just as she does now if she gets hurt. She was not numb to feelings because she was born early, and the same goes for babies in the womb. Babies killed in abortions feel everything -- every prick, every pull.

Shortly after birth, even Gabrielle's personality was displayed. Gabrielle pulled out her ventilator when she was 3 weeks old. By comparison, that would have been 32-33 weeks in gestational age. We could see on her face she did not like the ventilator, and it bothered her, and one night, she pulled it out. That was the turning point in raising our precious, strong-willed child. Even the nurses told us she would have a strong personality if she did that before she was supposed to be born!

Pregnant women will tell you they can tell a lot about their child by how they act in the womb. Some move around all the time, while some barely move. Some kick and do somersaults, while others are calm, and you hardly notice they are there. God's girls, don't believe the world's view on abortion. The Bible tells us that God knows us before we are even born, and God knows we are precious babies with a purpose and a destiny, not blobs!

Some interesting facts:

•There were 200,420 abortions among 15 though 19 year-olds in 2006. (4)

•27 percent of pregnancies among 15 through 19 year-olds ended in abortion in 2006. (4)

•The reasons teens give most frequently for having an abortion are: concern about how having a baby would change their lives, inability to afford a baby now and feeling insufficiently mature to raise a child. (4)

If you have had an abortion, you need to know God forgives you. You do not need to live under condemnation, because Christ has come to set us free. We do not have to live under the lies of the enemy. Later in chapter 9, we are going to hear from a woman who had an abortion. As you read her story, you too, can experience the powerful forgiveness of our loving God.

5. Used and left broken-hearted

You slept with him, left your virginity with him, and now the deal is off. He got what he wanted, and now you are left empty and thrown out like trash. This is the feeling many girls experience after breaking up with someone they have been intimate with. Being intimate is like putting two pieces of tape together face to face and then trying to pull them apart. There is going to be no way to separate the tape without chunks of the tape missing as they are permanently stuck together. That tape represents your emotions. There is no going back; you will never be able to look at him the same again.

I want you to share the gift of purity to your husband so you do not have to take memories and baggage with you into your marriage. Sometimes it can be hard for women to forget past experiences, and her husband is the one who gets robbed, because she cannot connect with him while remembering the past. It can cause communication, connection and intimacy problems in your marriage for many years to come. When the gift of purity has been opened, it cannot be rewrapped without wrinkles and irreversible damage apart from God's forgiveness.

I like that Facebook allows you to connect with people you have known throughout the experiences in your life. Some experiences I do not want to relive, like high school and my big hair days. Other times it is fun to remember an era of my life I would have forgotten. Recently, I have become friends with a few of the guys I had crushes on at various times in my life. It is fun to see what they are doing now and to see their families. The key for me is I was not intimate with them and being Facebook friends with them is not painful. It is pleasant to see where they are now without painful emotional memories. Remember we talked about not dating and being friends with guys because down the road you either have a trail of broken emotions and painful memories or a bunch of friends? I pray you will have lots of friends.

The Bible says in Numbers 32:23, "But if you fail to do this, you will be sinning against the Lord; and you may be sure that your sin will find you out." If you choose to sleep around, unfortunately, there will be consequences. They may come next week when you find out you are pregnant, or they may develop years down the road when the consequences of your sins finally catch up with you.

Discussion Questions

1. Is the risk of these consequences worth having "pleasure for a season?"
2. Who in your life can you learn from that has experienced one of these consequences?
3. Why do you think your friends (or you) ignore the warnings and sleep around anyway?

See No Evil, Hear No Evil

~~~~

"Finally, brothers, whatever is true, whatever is noble, whatever is right, whatever is pure, whatever is lovely, whatever is admirable — if anything is excellent or praiseworthy — think about such things."
Philippians 4:8

I am not one to stick my head in the sand, never go to a movie, throw out my television and live in a convent, but I examine what I watch, read and listen. Not everything the world produces is good material for Christians. I am not going to tell you "Do not watch this," or "Do not listen to this," but I want to lay out some guidelines and thinking points for you to consider as you make your own decisions. We all need the Word of God and the Spirit of the living God inside of us to give us direction.

A pastor friend of mine in California used to say to his children, "You can watch what we watch, drink what we drink and say what we say." In other words, in our family, there are no "adult" drinks, "adult" movies or things "adults" say. He said "If things are inappropriate for children, they are inappropriate for me."

Since hearing those words I have pondered why some things are for "adults only?" The answer may be because they are not meant for the innocent; they are not meant for the pure. If children saw them, they may have nightmares, because they are not yet desensitized to evil. Personally, even as an adult, I never want to be desensitized to evil. I want my spirit to be checked when the Holy Spirit is grieved.

Matthew 10:16 says, "I am sending you out like sheep among wolves. Therefore be as shrewd as snakes and as innocent as doves."

Jesus spoke these words as He was sending out the twelve disciples to preach. There are two powerful analogies for us in this verse. First, we need to know the world around us is like a bunch of wolves, ready to pounce on us at any moment. Most of the time, they are not there to be our friend. We know some of them will get saved and will become followers of Christ, but most of them are only there as wolves, ready to entrap us, just like sin. Magazines, television shows, movies, books, videos and all sorts of other media are attempting to fill us with "worldly ways."

The second analogy from this verse is the wisdom God has given us to discern right from wrong, yet at the same time remain innocent. We do not have to watch every movie, television show and YouTube video to be relevant and in touch with our culture. We want to remain innocent of evil. We do not need to try it to know it is wrong. I do not need to watch a movie I know is filthy to know that I should not watch it. I hear people say, "I need to listen to worldly music so I know how to relate to today's kids." However, I feel I do not need to saturate myself with sin to relate to sinners. I want to remain innocent.

John 15:19 says, "If you belonged to the world, it would love you as its own. As it is, you do not belong to the world, but I have chosen you out of the world. That is why the world hates you."

If your friends want to go to a movie and you have nothing else going on, what should you do? Before you answer, I would go to the Internet and read more about what messages the movie contains. There are many great Web sites that will reveal exactly how many swear words the film contains, how much violence is involved, and other inappropriate parts in that movie. One of those sites is Screenit.com., or you can sign up to receive movie reviews e-mailed to you from the Motion Picture Association, the organization that determines actual content ratings. The organization's website is www.mpaa.org or www.filmratings.com. If you truly desire to "see no evil" you may have to a skip a movie or go to a different one.

I love funny movies, but it is hard to find a good, clean funny show. From time to time there will be one showing and it is a treat to go see it. We, as a family, can laugh and enjoy the movie knowing we have already checked its content to know if it is clean. I would rather go to a clean movie fewer times than go to others that send me repenting the rest of the night.

Music is another area in which you have to decide what is healthy. There maybe a lot of information available for you to review before you buy a CD or download it on iTunes to help you. I love worship music as it is a blessing to fill our home and car with songs that glorify the Lord. It keeps our spirits lifted and our minds on God.

Do you know God made music for His glory? We were made to have fellowship with God and to worship Him through music. He made music for Himself. The devil is jealous of the worship God receives and wants worship for him. He has made the world's music to worship him and glorify sins. Music with swear words, lyrics about sex or shooting people does not come from God.

Our girls attended a one-day cheerleading camp for a local basketball team we have near our home in Sioux Falls. At the basketball game they performed a cheer/dance to a young female artist's song. I was familiar with who she was, and I knew young girls listened to her music, so we went to YouTube and looked up her music videos. I was shocked, because it was no better than the other mainstream music videos. I was angry, because it was not innocent and it was not clean, and I for sure did not want my children thinking moving that way was OK in our home. My girls will not be listening to her music.

As a result of this incident, we have found some Christian artists with music that glorifies God. Our girls can listen to that music and have fun dancing and glorifying the Lord. I know this may be extreme, but I am raising two precious girls who need to know there is a difference between us and the world. We will not bow to the idols the world bows to; we will worship Jesus in our home. Joshua 24:15 says, "As for me and my house, we will serve the Lord." The best part of all is that our girls are starting to write their own songs, and they can choreograph dances to their own original songs.

Psalm 101:2-4 says, "I will be careful to lead a blameless life…I will walk in my house with blameless heart. I will set before my eyes no vile thing…Men of perverse heart shall be far from me; I will have nothing to do with evil."

In this verse, the psalmist David is setting boundaries for himself. David is determined to be blameless and pure before the Lord, and he says he will be careful. He wants to be able to be in his home in peace, not tormented by the sins he has committed. We need to be like David and not allow any vile thing in front of our eyes. Maybe that means taking the television out of your room so you are not tempted or that may mean putting the computer out in the open so your parents and friends can see what you are viewing. How determined are you to set yourself up for success? Instead of seeing how much of the world we can take in and still be pure and innocent, we should say like David did that I will have nothing to do with evil. I will not watch it. I will not listen to it. I will not mess around with it and see how far I can go before I get bit.

Philippians 4:8 says, "Finally, brothers, whatever is true, whatever is noble, whatever is right, whatever is pure, whatever is lovely, whatever is admirable — if anything is excellent or praiseworthy — think about such things."

As young women of the Lord, we find ourselves constantly surrounded by the world and the anti-Christian message it promotes, and as a result, our minds think on those things. How can we be thinking about true, noble, right, pure, lovely, admirable attributes when worldly things are all around us? The reality is, Christians can find ourselves thinking more about boys, romance, violence, swear words, fantasy and evil far more than the things we should be. How can we think on pure things when the world around us is not pure? Where do true, noble, right, pure, lovely and admirable things come from? They come from God, and we need to be reading the Word of God, praying and spending time in fellowship with those who will build us up instead of the things this world has to offer that will tear us down.

Some of these things are a lot easier said than done. However, you have control over what you watch and what you listen to. You can decide what books to read, movies to attend, music to listen to, TV shows to watch, video games to play and what Internet sites to visit. If Jesus would not watch it with you, then you probably should not be watching it. Some of you may need to take some time and clean out your iPod, DVD collection, books, etc., and ask God to help you think on these things.

> How can we think on pure things when the world around us is not pure?

Discussion Questions

1. How is your entertainment library? Is it pure or does it need some cleaning?

2. How can you stand up to your friends when they want to see a movie you know is not appropriate?
3. Have you set standards and boundaries for yourself in regards to what you will watch and listen to?

Part 3
When God's Girl Is Hurt

When God's Girl Is Hurt

Part I

~~~~~~

"So if the Son sets you free, you will be free indeed." John 8:36

Molestation, rape and sexual abuse are extremely tough topics to talk about, but I want to deal with them. I want to talk to you girls as if I were talking to my own daughters, because they too will be reading this in just a few short years. This chapter could save some of you the pain of being hurt, for others it will offer healing if you have already been hurt from domestic abuse.

I wonder why little girls are molested and raped in untold numbers? Why are women told to be aware of men in parking lots who could rape and kill them? Why does the pornography industry make so much money and ruin many lives and marriages? Why are there thousands of men locked in our prisons and thousands more who should be because of sex crimes? Why are priests being found guilty for molesting little boys? (Some of these same issues can apply to women, too.)

There may not be any one reason, but the sexual society we live in has made it harder for guys to stay pure and even easier for them to act on the feelings they have. Television and movies, especially pornography, have made men aggressive and more likely to act out on what they have seen.

Men are visual, which means that they are easily turned on by images in a magazine or on a screen. Women, on the other hand, tend to be more emotional, meaning they may not be turned on by sight, but by feeling close through physical touch, combined with talking and communicating. You may hear guys say women are "so complicated" and this may help you understand why they would feel that way.

There are many words that describe sexual misconduct. I want to define a few of those words that you will hear on the news, at school, among your friends and in this chapter. At times I have been unsure what some of these terms meant when I have heard them.

Molestation is the act to bother, interfere with or annoy; to make indecent sexual advances to; or to assault sexually. The word assault means to attack physically. In other words, when you hear that someone has been molested that means someone has touched them inappropriately and may or may not have had intercourse with them. Molest is a very broad term.

The second word is rape, any act of sexual intercourse forced upon a person. Statuary rape is sexual intercourse with a girl under the age of consent, which varies in different states.

Sexual abuse is any form of touching sexually or intercourse that is not mutual and was forced upon a person. Often it can be violent and traumatic.

Some statistics report that 25 percent of women were sexually abused when they were children. Ninety percent of the time the molesters know their victims and have a relationship with them. The chance that some guy is going to jump into your car in a parking lot and rape you is much lower than the relatives that come at Christmas and special events, and we do not need to be scared or alarmed but aware and alert to what can happen.

You are a precious young girl and if anyone touches you in an inappropriate way you need to run, yell, scream and make a big scene. You need to tell another safe adult, and if they do not believe you, go to another adult such as a police officer. It does not matter if the molester told you not to tell. It is not acceptable, and you do not have to be a victim!

I have a friend who was molested by her father from the time of her earliest memories until she was 12 years old. Her story grieves me and makes me angry at the sin of this world. I have asked her to share her story with you for several reasons.

1. Through telling her story she is revealing the darkness that kept her bound for so long. She is no longer a slave to this wretched secret.

2. If you have been molested, we want you to know you are not alone. If you have not told an adult we want to give you permission to do so. If you have told an adult and are in the healing process we want you to know you are not alone and there is hope and peace.

> I was molested by my father from as young as I can remember.

3. You are still young, and there may be men who try to take advantage of you. If this happens to you, get out of the situation as quickly as possible and tell an adult. We want you to know you do not have to stay and you can leave the situation.

This is her story.

I was molested by my father from as young as I can remember. The earliest I can say is at about 3 years old. It continued until I was around 12 years old. Growing up with such perversion, I had no idea this was wrong until later in life. I assumed, as a young girl, that this was normal, because it was the only "acceptance" I received from my father. To me this is what love looked like. In order to feel loved by my father, as a little girl, I had to submit to the abuse, because it was either receive love in an unhealthy way or be completely rejected when I did not submit to the abuse. As I grew older, I began to be filled with shame, and I felt that somehow this abuse was my fault and I had brought this upon myself.

As a result of the abuse I began to hide behind the feeling that if anyone found out they would accuse me of putting myself in that situation and that I should have known better. I assumed that others were going to judge me, act differently toward me and label me. Additionally, my father made me feel like I was the one who was doing something wrong, not him. I felt if I told anyone that they wouldn't believe me and then, I assumed, they would reject me too. The trap of lies held me in bondage.

Around the age of 12, the molestation stopped, because I suspect he was afraid of physical consequences, and I was becoming old enough to realize it was wrong and tell someone what was happening. At the same time my body was changing into a young woman; I was learning about marriage, and I realized that this was wrong. Even though the sexual abuse stopped, the physical and emotional abuse did not. There was an instance when, in the midst of an argument, I asked him to stop treating me this way. He told me to stop talking back to him, that he could do what he wanted - then hit me. Whenever he was around, it was do what he said and do it now or you would get hit. It is hard to break off this type of emotional control.

Because of the abuse and the death of my mother, the relationship with my father had become that of a confidant and very hard to break from because he "needed" me, and I felt accepted being "needed." At the same time I was still continuing to be abused. Since he no longer could physically or sexually abuse, he would emotionally abuse me by holding whatever he could over my head. I would get a guilt trip from him if I didn't go to his house for a break while in college or do what he thought I should do or told me to do. In high school he threatened to send me to a new school, in college he would threaten to take my vehicle away. I could never make my own decisions; it was all about constantly pleasing him.

In order to cope with the lifetime of abuse, to gain acceptance, I began to pour myself into my schooling. In high school, it was an outlet in which I began to find comfort as I started to excel and others around me began to accept me as the smart one. It also meant that there was less contact with my father, as I would be involved in school activities or schoolwork. Additionally, in college and graduate school I continued to excel in my schooling to make sure that I was accepted so I didn't have to admit to being abused.

I attended a private Christian college that had chapel every week. At times, the speaker would give altar calls for those who were abused to come forward or seek help through the counseling department. I never responded because I did not want to admit that the abuse had happened. I did not want to deal with it. Once again, I thought I was trapped, because if I admitted this happened, then I would be questioned on why I didn't tell anyone and would have more shame and rejection, because I was wrong in not telling anyone what happened while it was happening. Why didn't I get out? Why didn't I tell?

After graduate school, the Lord led me back to Omaha. I was not ready after seven years of living away from home to return to the place of the abuse. However, I was obedient and through this, at age 26, God opened the doors for me to begin the healing process. I attended an International House of Prayer event and each person was given words of knowledge and encouragement. Those messages opened my heart to realizing that I needed to tell someone about what had happened to me.

That following Father's Day, I heard a message about the Father's love, and I realized that I did not know that kind of love from a father. That message began to open up a little more of my hard heart. Later that summer, I was asked to give my testimony at a Bible study. I realized while preparing that I needed to be honest about all of my testimony, including the abuse. I told my story and after the Bible study, one of the girls attending told me she had a similar story and told me about a great counselor who had helped her and could help me work through these issues. A few weeks later, I told the counselor my story for the first time in my life, and at age 26, I admitted that I was abused, something I had been trying to bury for my entire childhood.

Part of the healing process was to let my siblings know. Two of them said they were molested one time by our dad. The other one was not. All of us were physically and emotionally abused, so each of us has been supportive and having each other is what has helped us all to heal. Just having someone who understands the darkness of our childhood has been healing.

I have been able to date recently where before I was not even whole enough to know how to trust a man. My dad had not allowed me to date in high school, because he said all guys wanted was sex so why bother hanging out with them? I know God is my healer and being able to share my story with you has helped me to turn this bad thing into something good to help other young ladies. Please feel free to contact me through Rachel's e-mail, jerandrach@hotmail.com, if you need someone to talk to. ~

When God's Girl Is Hurt
Part 2

~~~~

We are going to spend one more chapter on the topic of molestation since it is a prevalent issue in our society. I want to have one more of my friends tell her story. I know Jordan and her love for the Lord; it is hard for me to imagine what she went through as a child. Her story shows me how God can literally change a person. When we allow Christ to come into our lives, He can break bondages that have held us captive for years. No matter what you have gone through, Christ can heal the past and set you free from the lies. You can be whole again.

This is Jordan's story.

This is what I remember and how I remember it. I was first molested by my sister's best friend's brother. My parents would let my sister and I go over to their house to play, and he and I would "play" together. He literally made it into a game, a kind of "house" game that was a secret. It was fun and felt good both physically and emotionally. I never felt bad, or like he was hurting me, but I had no idea it was wrong. I believe it went on my whole year of kindergarten, because I distinctly remember him saying, "When you get into first grade then we'll have sex." Thank God he moved that summer.

One day I broke the most important rule, and I told a friend about the "game." As it turns out she had played this game, too, and I was taught the wrong way to play the game, so she showed me the right way. Turns out, several people played this game. Then one night I couldn't sleep, and I sat in the hall of our house watching the pornography my parents had playing in the living room and realized this was something grown-ups really did do, it was "house." Here is by far the hardest thing ever, I then taught the "game" to my cousin.

I don't remember how, but I eventually did learn what it was and that it was wrong, and this led to the most horrible feeling in the world. I thought I was a child molester for teaching my cousin and that I was a homosexual, because I played it with girls. To top it all off my parents were physically abusive so I did not let anyone touch me for about six years. I would not be alone with other girls because I didn't want it to ever happen again, and I did not want to be gay. It became such an overwhelming horrible thing that I eventually blocked all of it from memory. I didn't know why I couldn't be touched or alone with people; I would just freak out for no reason. I actually did not remember that any of it had even happened until I was a sophomore in high school. I could not even hear the word molested without getting irate.

What I remember most about attending a purity conference was being so angry, holding on to a secret of having been molested and feeling robbed and dirty. Everyone talked about holding onto your purity and I sobbed thinking "MINE WAS STOLEN!!! IT'S NOT FAIR!! I DIDN'T HAVE A CHOICE!!!"

> I thought if I told anyone they would view me as the poor dirty little girl.

When I finally shared my secret, people would say, "It's not your fault," but to be honest that meant nothing because it didn't fix the problem, it didn't give me back what I thought was my purity nor did it give back my cousin's purity, and that was my fault. I taught her. She was younger than I was and I taught her. Therefore, I became a molester in my mind.

What a magnificent plan Satan had, as this one thing began affecting almost every area of my life. I didn't trust people; I didn't believe anyone would protect me; I thought if I told anyone they would view me as the poor dirty little girl - or even worse a child molester - and I hated myself for letting it happen.

The event that finally turned my life around was a soaking time of prayer. I basically sat in a room with two other women and they prayed for God to show me where I needed healing and forgiveness, and to forgive. I always knew God saw every moment of my life, and I was so ashamed that he saw what had happened, but I realized he was not mad; he was just as hurt as I was by it. That is where the healing began.

By the grace of God and His cleansing blood, I learned that the past was covered and forgotten and from this new moment on I could choose to stay "true". I say true and not pure because I still had a warped view of the word pure. I did not view myself as pure, but I knew I had not had sex and so I fought for my virginity. It was a battle, but I felt like it was all I had left to offer my husband. I could stay true in this area to him and the Lord. ~

I appreciate Jordan sharing these very deep issues that she had to deal with as a young lady. Perhaps you can relate to some of what she experienced. If you need someone to talk to you can contact her through my e-mail, jerandrach@hotmail.com. Jordan would love to pray with you and encourage you.

If you have been molested, there is help available. You can get in contact with a local church that has a staff counselor, or if your city has a counseling center they can help you work through these issues. Another option is to call the Rape, Abuse and Incest National Network (RAINN). They have a National Sexual Assault hotline available 24 hours a day, and you can talk to a counselor completely confidentially. They do not have your phone number or name unless you give it to them. Their toll-free number is 1-800-656-HOPE.

Discussion Questions

1. What are some signs that the situation you are in is not safe and you could get hurt?
2. How can you get out of a situation you realize is not safe?
3. How can you encourage those who have been hurt by rape or molestation?

Part 4
When God's Girl Sins

The Deadly Price Tag Of Sin

~~~~

"For you created my inmost being; you knit me together in my mother's womb. I praise you because I am fearfully and wonderfully made; your works are wonderful, I know that full well. My frame was not hidden from you when I was made in the secret place. When I was woven together in the depths of the earth, your eyes saw my unformed body. All the days ordained for me were written in your book before one of them came to be." Psalm 139:13

One of the hardest parts of writing a book on purity for teen girls is we have to talk about abortion. I cannot think very long about abortion without getting mad and frustrated considering the modern society we live in. It does not seem possible we can call abortion anything but killing. More than any other time in history, and more than most nations on earth, we have the technology to see babies from the moment they are conceived until the moment they are born. We know day by day what is happening in the mother's womb. Pregnancy is no longer the mystery it once was before fancy imaging equipment. When you are pregnant and an abortion clinic tells you that what is inside you is not alive, it is an outright lie.

If something is alive, in order for it to not be alive any more you have to kill it. What does it mean to be alive? If something is alive, it is growing, can reproduce and is always changing. Are rocks alive? No, because they do not grow and do not reproduce. Although water and rocks are in nature, they are not alive. But trees, grass and animals are alive because they grow, reproduce and change from young to old. The same goes for people. We know a baby is alive inside its mother's womb, because it is growing and changing. If we do not kill it and there is no complication at birth, it is going to be born and continue growing and changing until his or her appointed time of death. It is alive and will continue to be alive until someone aborts the process. Thus, the term abortion!

I have a friend, Riley, who had an abortion years ago when she was a teenager. I have asked her to share her story with you. I hope you will read carefully the words that she has written and allow her words to minister to you.

This is Riley's story.

While not all of my teen years were bad, the hardest parts of growing up were the overwhelming feelings I had that I wanted to feel loved. I think I felt this way because while my Dad tried to be a good father, he stopped hugging me when I was about 12 years old. I think he was afraid of me growing up into a woman, and he felt uncomfortable. But the only thing I thought was that there must be something wrong with me.

You see, my Dad had been brought up in an abusive home, which made him prone to angry, angry outbursts that terrified my mother, brother, sister and me. His unpredictable, moody behavior, along with not hugging me anymore, made me think I was a bad person, even though I hadn't done anything wrong. Many times I asked myself what it was that I did to make him so angry and say hurtful things. Now I know that he was dealing with severe hurts of his own. Hurting people hurt people. To make matters worse, he and my mother would argue about me, which made me feel like I was the reason for all the fighting that went on between them. While my mother would try to stick up for me when she thought my Dad was being unfair, in the end he always won the arguments.

During the summer after my sixth-grade year, our family experienced two family deaths that changed us forever. I believe that's when things got even worse. Still, I kept getting straight A's at school and tried desperately to be a Christian girl. I cannot hide that I was very angry at God for my aunt and grandma's deaths. My mother cried a lot and got very, very skinny. My dad's behavior was even worse during this time. I hated to see my mom so sad. And I would cry myself to sleep at night, because I wanted someone to hold me.

I lost my virginity when I was 17 to a boy I was sure I would marry. That is how I validated sleeping with him: I would marry him so it would be OK biblically. I even stayed in an abusive relationship with him for three years, because I wanted to make it right. However, everything went wrong, and we broke up.

Following that time, I rebelled against God and partied a lot in college. I didn't sleep with a lot of guys like many of my friends, but I did do drugs. And then, one stupid mistake, it happened. I was pregnant.

When I found out, I couldn't believe it. The first thing I thought was, "I have to get it out of me! My father will kill me! Plus, if it is a baby already, it won't be normal because of all the partying and drugs!" My friend helped me set up an appointment at Planned Parenthood. I do not remember much about the abortion, but I do remember them being very nice to me and telling me it was a "clump of tissue," and I would be all right. They also told me to ignore the protesters outside. I had to be at the clinic most of the day, and I recall it was very painful.

Six months later I met my husband. Married to him for 17 years now, he went through the grieving and guilt I felt years after the abortion. After my first son was born, I hit rock bottom about the abortion. I had become my father: Moody, sad and hurtful. I did not like who I was, but fortunately I was able to get counseling from a post-abortion counseling center with my very patient, sweet husband.

While I know Christ has forgiven me, I still think about how old that baby would be right now. I wonder if it was a boy or a girl. I will always have the regret that I lost my virginity before marriage. It's not like in the movies; no one talks about the guilt and emptiness you feel afterward. I wish I would have known that there is such a thing as "secondary virginity," meaning that if you lose your virginity you can start over and be abstinent. I wish I would have been told that birth control devices/methods don't always work. Please don't let anyone tell you that is the case, because many girls get pregnant thinking that they are protected. I did. I also wish I would have seen the fetal models that crisis pregnancy centers have. Had I seen that or seen an ultrasound, I think my baby would be alive. Lastly, I regret that I couldn't give the gift of my virginity to my sweet, amazing husband. He loves me unconditionally to this day, faults and all, ups and downs, and that's what God wants for us. I have a lot of wishes and regrets. That is why I am in this book for you to read.

If my story sounds familiar, I would encourage you to do this: Find someone to talk to at church and pray with them. If you struggle with a relationship with your dad, the wisest thing I read or perhaps someone said to me was, "Your heavenly father can fill those voids and be the Daddy you need." Many churches today have counselors on staff that you can connect with and check in with. If they don't, ask them to refer you somewhere. Find a Godly mentor.

If you have already had an abortion, I would urge you to find a crisis pregnancy center. Most have post-abortion counseling. It saved my life and has helped me forgive myself. If you don't have that available to you, talk to your pastor or a good Christian mentor you trust.

Be good to yourself. Forgive yourself. Take it one day at a time. Jesus gave His life for you and there is nothing you could do to make God not love you. ~

If you need someone to talk to, Riley wrote her story to be there for others. You can e-mail her through my e-mail, jerandrach@hotmail.com.

Discussion Questions

1. Do you know anyone who has had an abortion?
2. What can you say to encourage a friend not to get an abortion?
3. What are the alternatives to abortion?

You Can Be Pure Again

~~~~~

"Therefore, if anyone is in Christ, he is a new creation; the old has gone, the new has come!" II Corinthians 5:17

I wish every girl had a purity story that they could be proud of, but life is not always perfect. The devil is always working overtime to bring us into temptation.

In writing this book, I asked some of the girls from our youth group in California to write and tell me their purity stories. I am proud of the many girls who have chosen a lifestyle of purity and dedication to the Lord. As I received other e-mails I have grieved knowing lies the enemy consumed them with. Romantic movies and books tell fairy tales of love and romance, I believe many girls are willing to give up everything just to experience the love that they think those movies and books have.

I have met girls through the years who are embarrassed to say they are 18 years old and have never been kissed. One of these girls in particular was obsessed with romantic movies, and I was not surprised when I learned she had practically given herself physically to a guy who she was not even dating simply because she wanted to be kissed and experience romance. The young lady wanted to reach that point so badly it did not matter who the guy was.

My friend, Chelsea, e-mailed to tell me she had not given herself away physically but regrets even kissing a guy in college, because they are no longer together anymore and now she has those memories that will go into the next relationship.

Another friend Kristi says, "I think it's important that girls understand that when you sleep with someone that you not only connect physically, but also emotionally, and that is so much harder to heal from than the physical connection or the loss of someone you think you loved or cared deeply for."

It was interesting to hear their stories. I want you to hear from those who are walking just a few steps ahead of you and listen to what they are saying about the consequences of their choices, whether positive or negative.

Have you ever heard girls say, "We are going to get married so it is OK to sleep together?" Did you ever think why you would want to marry a guy that is pressuring you to sleep with him? Is that really the kind of man you want to be with the rest of your life? If he is willing to break God's laws now, will he not break them in the future? If he does not respect you now, he probably will not respect you later.

It was a priority to me to marry a man of God who would lead our family in the ways of the Lord. As you learned earlier, I ran away from the guys who wanted to use me for their own selfish needs. You need to do that too. No matter how long you have dated and how cute he is, if he is pressuring you to cross boundaries, then you may need to break up with him. The pressuring probably is not going to mysteriously stop; he is going to keep trying until he breaks you down.

Youth pastors spend a lot of their time trying to discourage teenagers from sleeping together and on the other hand, senior pastors and marriage counselors try to keep married people from getting divorced. Teenagers try so hard to be together, sneaking around their parents rules and trying to find places to be together, but once people get married we have to work ruthlessly to keep them from getting divorced! Why this reversal? One answer to this issue may be that marriage is more than sex, it is a relationship where two people are making decisions, living side by side, working jobs, raising kids, going through struggles, dealing with sickness, tragedy and numerous other issues. You will not be making out all day long in constant marital bliss.

Maybe, instead of spending your time figuring out how you are going to make out again, you should be talking, forming a relationship and building one another up to have good character. That way, if you do not marry this guy, at least you left him better than you found him, and you did not leave a torn piece of your heart with him.

What should you do if you are reading this book and you know kissing is nothing compared with where you have been - you have gone all the way with guys and you feel used and neglected? You know guys are discarding you like an old rag; you know you have sinned. I want you to know that God offers His love and forgiveness even though we have not earned or deserved it. Ladies, you can be pure again. Some call it "second virginity," others have different names, but it all comes from the forgiveness of almighty God.

I John 1:9 says, "If we confess our sins, he is faithful and just and will forgive us our sins and cleanse us from all unrighteousness."

Going back to our gift analogy, we cannot rewrap the gift without it being wrinkled and worn. But when Jesus rewraps the gift He takes out the wrinkles and makes it brand new again. He enjoys making us brand new!

If you have sinned in this area, or any other area, you can pause reading right now and confess your sins to God. You can have a fresh start, which the Lord lovingly offers to us. It is the beauty of forgiveness as Psalm 103:12 describes, "As far as the east is from the west, so far has he removed our transgressions from us."

To ask for forgiveness, you can pray a simple prayer by: (A) admitting you are a sinner and have done wrong, (B) Believing that Jesus is your Savior and ask Him into your heart and life, and (C) Confessing with your mouth that Jesus Christ is the Lord of your life. Tell someone, perhaps your mother or youth pastor, about your new found faith in Jesus! If you have asked Jesus into your heart before but have fallen away into sin, you too can rejoice that God has forgiven you as well.

> If you truly desire a change, God will give you the strength to live this new life for Him!

If you have asked Jesus to forgive you of your sins the Bible says in 2 Corinthians 5:17, "Therefore, if anyone is in Christ, he is a new creation; the old has gone, the new has come!" You are a new person. God does not remember your sin, because it is covered by the precious blood of Jesus. The Bible says in Luke 15:7, "I tell you that in the same way there will be more rejoicing in heaven over one sinner who repents than over ninety-nine righteous persons who do not need to repent." All heaven is rejoicing with your decision to follow Christ. You are clean and in right standing with God; it is something to rejoice about.

God does not magically erase our memories of the past, but He gives us leaders and spiritually-motivating books like this one to help us set new boundaries and a new walk of purity. If you truly desire a change, God will give you the strength to live this new life for Him!

My husband, Jeremiah, was not a virgin when I met him, and that was not easy for me. It took me a while to figure out if he could really be the person God had for me since he had not waited for me. As I meditated in God's presence, God revealed to me it was a lifestyle of sin Jeremiah was living in the past and was covered by the blood of Jesus once he asked Christ into his life. Once Jeremiah became a Christian, his life changed. He no longer desired to be promiscuous. Most of his high school classmates did not believe him, but after they saw him following through on his word, they knew he was for real. It came at a cost, however. He lost most of his friends when he decided to follow Jesus, because he would not do the things they did any longer. When Jeremiah broke up with his girlfriend, she could not believe she was dumped for Jesus! She ridiculed him and spread nasty lies about him. Jeremiah knew the decision to follow Christ was worth the slight persecution he endured.

When we started dating a year after he got saved, we set very high standards and never crossed the line. We dated for three years; on our wedding night, I was a virgin and Jeremiah was pure in the eyes of the Lord.

There are some very practical things that you can do to help you live this life of purity. The Bible says in 1 Corinthians 10:13, "No temptation has seized you except what is common to man. And God is faithful; he will not let you be tempted beyond what you can bear. But when you are tempted, he will also provide a way out so that you can stand up under it." One way to help yourself is to not put yourself in the place of temptation.   For you, that may mean not going certain places you know you cannot handle. Talk about your boundaries out loud with a parent or a friend, and have a clear understanding of where they are. I was bold from the beginning with Jeremiah, because I was proud to be a virgin and would be one on my wedding night. I had no doubt. I was never pressured by him in any way, because we understood where the boundaries were.

Picture a guy putting a girl on a pedestal. They look up to the girls they like, but the guy also likes to test the girl on the pedestal to see if she can be shaken off. If she can be shaken, then he can use her to please his own sensual desires, if she cannot be shaken, then he really looks up to her and she gains his respect. If I would have come off the pedestal for Jeremiah we may not be married today, because we both wanted to marry a person of character. We need to not come off the pedestal for anyone!

Discussion Questions

1. Is it really possible to be pure again?
2. What boundaries and standards should you set for your relationships?
3. How can you keep yourself on the pedestal?

Part 5
Taking Care Of God's Girl

Is Drinking For God's Girl?

~~~~

"Do not get drunk on wine, which leads to debauchery. Instead, be filled with the Spirit." Ephesians 5:18

In this part of the book we are going to detour around sexual purity and discuss a few other ways you can stay pure outside of sexual areas. These next topics can hurt you physically and mentally and even lead to long-term damage to your body and untold consequences to your life.

The Bible says in I Corinthians 6:19, "Do you not know that your body is a temple of the Holy Spirit, who is in you, whom you have received from God? You are not your own." This means if you have accepted Jesus Christ as your Savior, the Holy Spirit has chosen you to abide in. The God of the universe has chosen your feeble physical body in which to make His home and dwelling place on this earth. The matter is not to be taken lightly, and you can avoid a lot of pain in this life if you will treat your body as the temple of the Lord. You belong to Him, ladies, you are God's girl!

101

In every area of life we have choices. Choices are what make us unique and individual. Some choices do not really matter, like what type of ice cream you prefer, while some matter for a lifetime. One area of disagreement amongst Christians is whether a single glass of wine or beer will hurt them? Should Christians drink alcohol? Here is how I see it, I am afraid those who choose to drink alcohol innocently justify opening a tiny crack into the world of alcohol use, not understanding that the crack they have opened will not stay small. So the question I pose is why allow that little crack in the foundation when there is a lot to lose?

The Bible was written hundreds of years ago, and it warns us of the dangers of being drunk. Ephesians 5:18 says, "Do not get drunk on wine, which leads to debauchery. Instead, be filled with the Spirit." Hundreds of years after these words were written there are still alcoholics and drunkards. Many even claim to be Christians. Why? These men and women have chosen not to listen to warnings and were deceived into thinking one drink would not hurt. Their justification goes from a single drink to two, and then unintentionally becoming drunk. Step by step, people compromise. What begins as just one drink can take over their lives. Then one day they wake up an alcoholic, bound by the very thing they thought they had control of!

I am reminded of a story I once heard about a stage coach company who was looking to hire a driver to drive people through a very dangerous stretch of mountainous roads. One of the applicants got as close to the edge as possible to show how good he was at handling the horse without going over the edge. He held the people breathless as he avoided tumbling over the edge by a few mere inches. The other applicant stayed as close to the wall of the mountain as he could to put the passengers at ease and ensure they made it all the way to the top of the mountain with plenty of room for error. Which man do you think got the job? The one who was not afraid of the edge and wanted to show his skills in avoiding going over the mountain edge or the one who stayed close to the wall and allowed himself room for error? The man who got the job was the one who stayed close to the wall.

This is the way many people approach alcohol and drinking. People know the Bible says to not get drunk with wine but they get as close to the line as possible and hope they make it without going over the edge. The next time they drink, they get a little closer to the edge, and so on, until they cross the line and finally give in and say, "What does it matter if I get drunk?"

Personally, I have chosen to not allow a crack in the fountain of my life and not ride the edge but rather to avoid alcohol all together. Proudly, I can say I have never tasted alcohol in my life, and it is sure a lot safer than ruining my life as a result of the damages alcohol can cause.

I have chosen this lifestyle as the effects of alcohol have damaged and destroyed lives. Some of you may know personally the pain perpetrated on you from an alcoholic. Alcoholics hurt themselves physically through the damage done to their bodies, and they hurt those around them emotionally. As you watch or read the news count the number of lives are hurt when alcohol is involved in car

103

accidents, domestic violence, fights, etc. Usually when there is an accident the first thing the police look for is alcohol use.

Here is only a partial list of some of the things alcohol can cause:

- Car accidents
- Date rapes
- Domestic violence: especially to women and children
- Fights: bars, home, etc
- Hangovers
- Loss of jobs
- Liver disease and other physical problems

Abovetheinfluence.com gives a really good description of some of the facts about alcohol. This will really help you put things into perspective.

What is Alcohol?

> Alcohol is created when grains, fruits or vegetables are fermented, a process that uses yeast or bacteria to change the sugars in the food into alcohol. Alcohol has different forms and can be used as a cleaner or antiseptic; however, the kind of alcohol that people drink is ethanol, which is a sedative. When alcohol is consumed, it's absorbed into a person's bloodstream. From there, it affects the central nervous system (the brain and spinal cord), which controls virtually all body functions. Alcohol actually blocks some of the messages trying to get to the brain. This alters a person's perceptions, emotions, movement, vision and hearing.

Listen, young ladies, it is not just a drink! It will change you, and you are not the same when you drink. Alcohol changes your blood, affects the central nervous system, and alters your perceptions, emotions, movement, vision and hearing.   To protect you, your family, your friends and your future, do not drink. Do not allow a small crack in the foundation of who you are. Avoid evil and things that can lead to evil. I pray this, because I love you, and I want you to be the very best person God intended for you to be. That means avoiding the traps the devil will lay out for you.

> It is not just a drink!!! It will change you, and you are not the same when you drink.

God's girl is one filled with the Holy Spirit, recognizing that she is the temple of the Holy Spirit. She desires to be a clean and holy vessel set apart for God. I choose to be filled with the Holy Spirit instead of a "spirit" the world offers me. Have you ever noticed a sign outside a liquor store that says "Beer, Wine and Spirits?" There is a spirit that comes with drinking, and it is not the Holy Spirit, even the liquor stores know that alcohol will fill you with a spirit that is outside of yourself.

No alcoholic set out to be one, they started with one drink. Alcoholism begins with a choice, but in the end it really becomes a disease and it controls the person, the person does not control or choose it.

Discussion Questions

1. Why do people drink?
2. Can a glass of wine hurt you?
3. Are there any benefits to drinking?

Is Smoking For God's Girl?

~~~~

*"Do you not know that your body is a temple of the Holy Spirit,
who is in you, whom you have received from God? You are not your
own." I Corinthians 6:1*

On the packaging of every cigarette carton is a
warning to smokers:

*"SURGEON GENERAL'S WARNING: Smoking
causes lung cancer, heart disease, emphysema, and may complicate
pregnancy. Quitting smoking now greatly reduces serious risks to your
health. Smoking by pregnant women may result in fetal injury,
premature birth, and low birth weight. Cigarette smoke contains carbon
monoxide"*

I Corinthians 6:19 says, "Do you not know that your
body is a temple of the Holy Spirit, who is in you, whom you
have received from God? You are not your own."

The fact that the creator of the universe would choose you as His dwelling place on this earth is incredible; He resides in you. God has dwelled several different places on earth. He used to reside in a pillar of cloud by day and pillar of fire by night while the Israelites were wandering in the wilderness. When the temple was built, His presence was seen in the Holy of Holies. After Jesus died on the cross and rose again, He ascended into heaven and God chose us as His dwelling place. We are now the place where God the Holy Spirit shows His glory. He no longer dwells in a tabernacle or temple but in us.

The Bible instructs us we are to take care of the temple where He dwells, as we are stewards of this temple. As you grow older, you will understand why being a good steward pays off. Those who do not eat right find it harder and harder to lose weight and stay healthy. Those who choose to use drugs, drink alcohol or become sexually promiscuous will see the result of their consequences often in the damage to their bodies. Even those who have been professional boxers now suffer Parkinson's disease as a result of their chosen lifestyle. No doing simple chores, like brushing your teeth, can harm you causing decay in your teeth and even creating the need for dentures later down the road.

Some people may say that smoking is a gray area, because the Bible does not specifically say to not smoke. However, it does not say not to suck on the tailpipe of a car either, but we know not to do that because of all the dangerous chemicals in the exhaust of our cars.

I am surprised with all the information available about smoking that teenagers still choose to pick up this habit. To get more insight into this subject for myself, I, again, asked my friend, Dr. Addison Tolentino, an oncologist (cancer doctor), to help me out. I asked Dr. Tolentino to see what he would say to young people about smoking in light of his experience as a cancer specialist. As it turns out, the cigarette ads and anti-smoking campaigns you see today are telling the truth!

"It is true that tobacco and tobacco smoke can cause cancer. Tobacco and its smoke contain at least 4,000 chemicals of which 55 are known carcinogens (which means cancer-causing chemicals). These chemicals can lead to DNA damage in human cells then cause cancer most commonly, lung cancer. BUT it can cause *fourteen* other cancer types as well," he said.

- Nasopharynx (behind the nose)
- Paranasal sinuses
- Oral cavity (mouth)
- Larynx (voice box)
- Esophagus
- Uterus
- Bladder
- Acute Myeloid Leukemia
- Nasal cavity (nose)
- Lip
- Pharynx
- Pancreas
- Kidney
- Stomach

Dr. Tolentino continues, "Smoking is not the only cause for these particular cancers but has been known to be a major contributor. I should also mention nicotine, which is an ingredient in cigarettes, does not cause cancer but makes a person addicted to tobacco. Smoking can also contribute to other diseases such as stroke, heart attack and lung diseases. In the United States alone, smoking kills 440,000 people each year – imagine, more than all of the people who died in the December 2009 earthquake in Haiti!"

So ladies, this is serious. The ads are not a propaganda scheme to keep you from doing something "fun" or "pleasurable," but simply a wise decision on your part as the keeper of the temple of the Lord. If a half a million people die a year from smoking, I think I will learn from those who have gone before me and stay away!

Our bodies were not made to have toxins put directly into them and still thrive. The Bible says in Psalm 139:14, "I am fearfully and wonderfully made." Our bodies are complex and so intricate that we still do not know everything there is to know even about the human body we live in. But with the things we do know, we would be wise to listen to those who study these issues and have seen the devastation that smoking can cause.

Obviously, the best choice for anyone who has smoked is to stop smoking, but even then sometimes the damage is already done. Dr. Tolentino told me of one lady who had stopped smoking more than 50 years ago but still developed lung cancer from the habit she had as a young woman.

The choice is yours. If you are offered a cigarette and told one will not hurt you, run! If you never start, you never have to stop. Most of us know people who have tried to stop and cannot. Advertising for helping people to stop smoking is everywhere, too, and should be taken into consideration. If it is so hard for people to stop, then maybe one will hurt you. A wise woman sees the danger and heeds the warning!

If you desire to stop smoking, there are endless possibilities out there on the Internet and in the stores. Do your research to see which ways work and which do not have a high success rate. You need to pray and ask God to release you of the desire to smoke and to give you wisdom as to which method will work for you.

Discussion Questions

1. Why do teenagers smoke?
2. What is the reason you or your friends have tried smoking?
3. Do you know someone who has tried to quit smoking? Why can't they stop?

Are Drugs For God's Girl?

~~~~~

"The acts of the sinful nature are obvious: sexual immorality, impurity and debauchery, idolatry and witchcraft [which includes the use of drugs]; hatred, discord, jealousy, fits of rage, selfish ambition, dissensions, factions, and envy; drunkenness, orgies, and the like. I warn you, as I did before, that those who live like this will not inherit the kingdom of God." Galatians 5:19-21

While we were youth pastors in California our youngest daughter, Gabrielle, was born in Omaha while we were home on vacation. She was born 10 weeks early, and I had to have a cesarean section. After the surgery, the doctors began giving me pain medicine. I was in serious pain and could hardly stand or walk for a few days, but because of the situation and all the decisions that I needed to make, I needed my brain to be quick and sharp. We were 24 hours away from home and needed to solve issues about how to care for our other daughter, Zoe, where we were going to live for a few

113

months, how we were going to get our car out of the airport and who was going to take care of our home in California all while being stuck in the hospital with a very critical baby. I remember the second day I asked the nurse if I could stop taking the pain medicine, because I could not stand my brain working so slow.

The medication I was given at the hospital is about my only encounter with drugs. Drawing from this experience I often wonder when I hear about people addicted to drugs, even pain killers, like I was taking in the hospital how they can stand not having their brains sharp and quick? It drove me crazy when I could not think fast.

Recently, my dentist prescribed Amoxicillin for an infection that I had. Within minutes of taking one dose I remember becoming tired and groggy, and I could barely stay awake. It was difficult, because I could not stop and sleep since I had my family to take care of. I wanted those pills to be gone so, again, I could have my brain back and not be so sleepy. Several of my friends said antibiotics do not cause you to be drowsy but when I did some research I found there were a lot of people who have that same reaction. This experience has proven to be a good teaching time for me to teach my girls about medicines and how they may solve one problem and be necessary to take, but there are always side effects when you take substances the body is not meant to have.

Ladies, one thing you do need to understand about what we call "street drugs" like cocaine and marijuana, is the reason drug dealers want you to do drugs is because it makes them money. It is all about the almighty dollar, and they may

114

not charge you the first time, but once you are hooked there is nothing you can do but come up with the money. For the drug dealer, it is not about feeling good or escaping reality, it is about money. If no one made money off of drugs, there would be no street drugs.

Maybe your friends are a different story. Why do your friends offer you drugs, maybe for acceptance? If you do drugs, your friends become validated in doing drugs, too. They do not feel bad, because you accepted them by joining in.

I know some of you may want to try drugs because you want to know what it is like, but how much better it is to say, "I do not need to try drugs?" I have never tried street drugs or prescription drugs not prescribed to me. It is a lot like alcohol, why open a door that does not need to be opened? We need to learn from those who have done addictive things and avoid it.

If you know something is unwise, why do you need to try it? My reason is, I am God's girl, and I belong to Him. My body is His temple, and I will allow no vial thing to touch me. Why not stay away? There was a commercial when I was growing up with a frying pan frying an egg in it. You could hear the egg sizzling in the grease then the ad would say, "This is your brain on drugs." The ad was portraying if you do drugs your brain will be "fried." I did not need to try drugs to know that the commercial was true. I heeded the warning and stayed clear.

Teen Challenge is a drug and alcohol rehabilitation program of the Assemblies of God. When I was growing up, a group would come to our church and tell their stories of young men and women caught in drug addiction, alcoholism and violence and how God delivered them. I would say to myself, "I am not going to do that, because then I would have to get set free from it. Why not just avoid it, and I do not have to go through the agony they talked about in their withdrawal phase?"

I talked to Dr. Brian Kidman, who has a family practice in Sioux Falls, he told me about the effects that drugs can have on people. "Depending on the drug used, a vast variety of health problems can occur, involving physical health (heart attacks, blood vessel disease, cancer, strokes, death, etc.), mental and emotional health (memory loss, schizophrenia, learning disabilities, depression, anxiety, phobias, etc.) and spiritual health (guilt, fears, demonic influence, strongholds, oppression, torment, suicide, etc.)," he said.

From time to time, in the news we have heard about celebrities and even a few of their children who have died of drug overdose and drug interactions. When we hear these stories, we need to realize drug use is serious. Though those pills look small and harmless, if too many are taken or the wrong combination gets in your system, your life is at risk - and you do not even realize it.

While in California, we held a Wednesday night service before Easter, and we played a video of the song "Mary Did You Know" by Mark Lawry put to the movie "The Passion of the Christ". It was a powerful video that my brother edited together especially for us. We were going to play it on Easter morning in the main service, but I felt compelled to play it in advance for the youth group. After we played it several teenagers gave their hearts to the Lord, including Nicole, who had grown up in the church but was not serving the Lord. She accepted Christ that night. The following Wednesday we got a call early in the morning that Nicole had died in her sleep from a drug interaction. The news jolted me to know that we had led her to the Lord only days before her appointment with God!

The autopsy revealed she died from drugs she was prescribed that had interacted with an over-the-counter medication. Situations like Nicole's happen either from street drugs, prescription drugs or over-the-counter drugs. Innocently, here was a beautiful girl who died from something so simple yet deadly.

> They both died with the video controllers still in their hands.

One other time in Susanville, there were two boys who got methadone from a girl who had started attending our youth group. She had stolen these drugs from a relative, and the boys bought it from her at their school's homecoming. That night the boys took it and were in the room of one of the boys playing video games when they both died with the video controllers still in their hands. The girl in our youth group was arrested and was sentenced to 11 years in prison. That was another time when the reality of drugs hit home for me. This situation ruined the life of this young girl, but I pray she finds her way back to the Lord.

We need to not be deceived into thinking our internal pain and hurts can be healed by a substance that is addictive and destructive. You may escape pain momentarily, but soon you will come down off that high and need to start all over again. If you use drugs to cover up physical or emotional pain - or drugs are the only lifestyle you know - there is still a way out.

If you have pain in your heart and think drinking or doing drugs is the answer, I dare you to cry out to Jesus. He is there, and He will hear you. Jesus longs to heal your heart and give you peace that you cannot even understand. He loves you and died on the cross for your sins; He will never leave you or forsake you. Take a moment and cry out to Him and allow His presence to be the healing you need instead of the false hopes that the world has to offer.

One of the highest-rated drug treatment centers in the United States is Teen Challenge. Their success rate is the highest you will find anywhere. Each center is a little different and accepts different ages and genders. These centers are a wonderful place to find healing and restoration in a biblically-sound environment. For those who want to be set free, Teenchallengeusa.com will help you locate a center that is right for you.

I want to show you something cool in the Bible. Did you know the Bible talks about drugs? The very words "pharmacy" and "pharmaceutical" come from the Greek word for sorcery.

Galatians 5:19-21says, "The acts of the sinful nature are obvious: sexual immorality, impurity and debauchery, idolatry and witchcraft [which includes the use of drugs]; hatred, discord, jealousy, fits of rage, selfish ambition, dissensions, factions, and envy; drunkenness, orgies, and the like. I warn you, as I did before, that those who live like this will not inherit the kingdom of God."

The word "witchcraft" in Galatians is also translated "sorcery" and refers to the use of drugs. The Apostle Paul calls witchcraft associated with drug use a sin and the non-medical use of drugs is considered one of the acts of the sinful nature. Using drugs, whether to get a high or to tap into the occult, is one of the sinful ways users demonstrate their depraved and carnal nature.

The Bible says again in Revelation 9:21, "Neither repented they of their murders, nor of their sorceries (pharmaceuticals), nor of their fornication, nor of their thefts."

Drugs were, in fact, an integral part of many ancient Near East societies. The pagan cultures surrounding the nation of Israel used drugs as part of their religious ceremonies. Both the Old Testament and New Testament condemn sorcery and witchcraft. In those days, drug use was tied to sorcery. Drugs were prepared by a witch or shaman and were used to enter into the spiritual world by inducing an altered state of consciousness, allowing demons to take over the mind of the user. In our day, many use drugs merely for what they call recreational purposes, but we cannot discount the occult connection.

The psychic effects of drugs should also not be discounted. A questionnaire designed by Charles Tate sent to users of marijuana documented some disturbing findings. In an article in "Psychology Today," he noted one-fourth of the marijuana users who responded to his questionnaire reported they were taken over and controlled by an evil person or power during their drug-induced experience. Over half of those questioned said they have experienced religious or "spiritual" sensations in which they met spiritual beings. (1)

Drug use is not just addictive but has ties to witchcraft and sorcery. My friends, we need to run from the things of this world. We need to avoid the temptations that the devil has laid out for us and instead listen to the Word of God with its warnings and guidance.

Discussion Questions

1. How would you or do you handle being approached by someone to do drugs?
2. Why do so many teenagers use drugs?
3. How do you feel about what the Bible says about drugs?

Part 6
Empowering God's Girl

He Has Got The Power

~~~~

"But you will receive power when the Holy Spirit comes on you; and you will be my witnesses in Jerusalem, and in all Judea and Samaria, and to the ends of the earth." Acts 1:8

    The best news that comes in trying to live a life of purity is we do not have to live it alone! God has given us the greatest gift in the Holy Spirit, because God knows that we are weak and cannot live a victorious life without Him.

    Just before Jesus ascended into heaven, He told the disciples to go into Jerusalem and wait for the Holy Spirit. Jesus knew we would need the Holy Spirit, so the disciples waited in the upper room and the Holy Spirit came upon them in a way they could never imagine.

    Acts 2:1-4 says, "When the day of Pentecost came, they were all together in one place. Suddenly a sound like the blowing of a violent wind came from heaven and filled the whole house where they were sitting. They saw what seemed to be tongues of fire that separated and came to rest on each of them. All of them were filled with the Holy Spirit and began to speak in other tongues as the Spirit enabled them."

To summarize the rest of the chapter, the people in Jerusalem, who were there from all over the world for Pentecost, heard the disciples speaking in their language, and they thought they must have been drunk. However, Peter stood up and told everyone that they were not drunk, but what they were experiencing had been prophesied by the prophet Joel. Peter explained to the onlookers that just days ago Jesus was crucified, but God had raised Him from the dead. The people were so moved by what Peter had spoken they asked what they needed to do. Peter told them they need to repent of their sins and accept Jesus into their hearts. In one day, 3,000 people believed and became Christians.

As you continue to read the book of Acts, and I encourage you to do so, it is exciting to see what the Holy Spirit did to change the lives of so many people. Many people were healed and set free from demons; some were saved in miraculous ways and given visions. But it did not come easy as some were ridiculed, thrown in prison and even stoned to death for following Christ.

The gift of the Holy Spirit, with the evidence of speaking in tongues, is the most wonderful gift I have been given outside of salvation. It gives me power to live for Christ! It edifies my spirit and strengthens me every day.

Mark 16:17-18 says, "And these signs will accompany those who believe: In my name they will drive out demons;

124

they will speak in new tongues; they will pick up snakes with their hands; and when they drink deadly poison, it will not hurt them at all; they will place their hands on sick people, and they will get well."

> The gift of the Holy Spirit, with the evidence of speaking in tongues, is the most wonderful gift I have been given since salvation.

I want to encourage you to read the book of Acts and see the cool things the new church did for Christ through the power of the Holy Spirit. The early church changed its world for Christ, and we are still benefitting from that obedience. The people were bold; they were brave; they healed the sick; they cast out demons. The disciples were filled with the Holy Spirit, and as a result, believed through Him they could do everything Jesus promised.

To God's girls, the Holy Spirit has many attributes. One of my favorites is that He is our counselor or teacher. How awesome to have a constant guide in your life. I sure need a constant counselor in my life.

John 14:26 says, "But the Comforter, which is the Holy Ghost, whom the Father will send in my name, he shall teach you all things, and bring all things to your remembrance, whatsoever I have said unto you."

This same verse says He is our comforter. As a teenager, I remember at times crying and being overwhelmed with life, but the Holy Spirit came into my life and comforted me. His still small voice would bring to my mind the scriptures that I had planted deep into my heart since I was a young girl. I know many of you need comfort with the pressures you are facing in life, and the Holy Spirit is there to give it to you.

To be baptized in the Holy Spirit comes from the Greek word baptein meaning to "steep, dye or color." A good example I like to use in being baptized in the Holy Spirit is like a cucumber becoming a pickle. When a cucumber is put into the yummy vinegar juice, it begins to change from its old life as a cucumber into its new life as a pickle. It will never be the same once it has been baptized. So with us, we will never be the same once we are baptized in the Holy Spirit. He wants to change us into something greater for His purpose.

There are many books written on the Holy Spirit if you want to study deeper about the wonderful things He does in our lives and for the church. By reading the New Testament, you will also see how the Holy Spirit used the first Christian church as a starting point for the rest of history.

One statement I want to leave you with in this chapter is in Acts 2 when Peter was standing before a large crowd on the day of Pentecost. He said to them, "Repent and be baptized, every one of you, in the name of Jesus Christ for the forgiveness of your sins. And you will receive the gift of the Holy Spirit. The promise is for you and your children and for all who are far off — for all whom the Lord our God will call." Ladies, this promise is for you and for me; all we need is to ask.

You can take a moment to pause and ask the Lord right now to fill you with His Holy Spirit and empower you to live this life of purity. God is gracious and desires to give good gifts to His children. I was filled with the Holy Spirit, with the evidence of speaking in tongues, at church camp when I was 10 years old. Since that time, I have been following Christ and praying every day in the Holy Spirit and encouraging others to do the same. We are weak, and we do not know how to pray, but the Holy Spirit is there for us.

Discussion Questions

1. Who is the Holy Spirit?
2. How can we rely on the Holy Spirit?
3. In what areas do you need the Holy Spirit's power?

It Is All About The Book

~~~~

"I have hidden your word in my heart that I might not sin against you." Psalm 119:11

Recently, Jeremiah and I have been dealing with a situation with an acquaintance who lives exactly opposite of purity. The family members are not Christians and do not want anything to do with God. They drink, smoke, do drugs, have sex outside of their marriage and are lost apart from God. We pray for them every day, and our girls take every opportunity to witness to their children. Recently, child protective services took their children for a few days, because they were not being taken care of. The couple is threatening a divorce, and their home is in turmoil.

The family has been completely torn apart. It is so sad, and it breaks my heart. I know you, too, probably have friends and family members who could be in a similar situation. The lure of the world, and what it says feels good and will satisfy, has left them empty and searching for something to fill the void in their lives. The world says that drinking and sex outside of marriage will make you happy and bring fulfillment, but in honesty, it makes you emptier inside, because you are living outside of God's plan.

As Christian young girls, you need to be very deliberate about learning the Bible and standing on the Word of God. We have a society void of the knowledge of the Word of God, and we don't know how to resist the devil, because the Word is not planted deep within us. When the devil comes at us with temptations and things of this world, he lures us in. We need to have the Bible hidden in our hearts and stand on those scriptures to help us in time of temptation.

Psalm 119:11 says, "I have hidden your word in my heart." But have we really? Are we continually learning Scripture and hiding it in our hearts? We need to be daily investing the Word of God deep in our hearts so, "That I might not sin against you." I do not want to sin against the Lord and do things that are not pleasing to Him, but I do not know right from wrong if I am not taught in the ways of the Lord.

Hiding the Word of God in our hearts is an ongoing process. We never will have it all treasured and can then stop learning. It is a continual process, girls. II Corinthians 10:12-13 says, "So, if you think you are standing firm, be careful that you don't fall! No temptation has seized you except what is common to man. And God is faithful; he will not let you be tempted beyond what you can bear. But when you are tempted, he will also provide a way out so that you can stand up under it."

After we hide God's Word in our hearts, we need to stand upon it. In other words, when problems come or temptations near, we can pull out the Word of God from our hearts and use those words to strengthen us through the trial. We need to literally cling to the Word and use the verses over again to remind ourselves, and the devil, what the Word of God says.

He wrote the book!

With our friends who have lost nearly everything, I am grieved, because I see what the devil can do to destroy families. I pray they can see how God's Word has the answers and direction for their lives. It encourages me to dig deeper into Scripture to improve my own family. I want to know how to be a better wife to my husband and how to be a better mother to my children. I want to cling to the words of Christ and know He loves us so much to give us His instructions to guide us, through His Word.

When Jesus said in John 10:10, "I have come that you might have life and life more abundantly," I believe He meant every word. By reading the Word and being a person who obeys Scripture, we can live at peace and love our neighbor; we are creating an abundant life.

Those that do not have Christ in their life and choose not to live according to the Bible create more problems for themselves. When we choose to go our own way, we do not have peace and can get in trouble with our friends, family and the law. We are tempted to justify our sins and wonder what happened to our abundant life. Well sisters, if we do not drink it will be hard to get in trouble with the law for driving drunk. If you do not have sex before marriage, you will not have to worry who the father of your child is.

God has an awesome plan for us, but we mess it up if we don't follow His plan. The results of disobeying His word will be with us the rest of our lives. He wrote the book! But, the best part is, He wrote it for us, because He knew we needed it.

Discussion Questions

1. Why did God give us the Bible?
2. What do we do when we do not want to agree with the Bible?
3. Why should we believe the Bible?

Part 7
Be God's Girl

Hot Topics

~~~~

"Do not be yoked together with unbelievers. For what do righteousness and wickedness have in common? Or what fellowship can light have with darkness?" II Corinthians 2:14

Hot Topic #1: Dating Non Christians

If I were to ask you if your boyfriend is saved and you have to pause and think about how to answer that, he might not be saved. If he has started to go to church mainly to be with you, he may not be a Christian. He could be interested in doing whatever it takes to be with you right now; if you break-up with him, he could have nothing to do with God once again.

The Bible describes dating and marrying a non-Christian to two oxen plowing in a field together. I know it is hard for us to imagine such a thing since most of us are not currently using oxen on a daily basis. However, picture in your mind two oxen yoked together. One is pulling left, and the other is pulling right. They would never be able to actually

135

go forward, because they are going from side to side. It is the same with dating a non-Christian. Your relationship cannot progress, because you are pulling each other's throats from side to side. If one of you tries to step forward, the other one gets their oxygen supply cut off, because the yoke is being pulled to the side and the front at the same time. Does that sound like what may be going on in your relationship?

Those of you that are dating non-Christians are going to have to make a decision to either stay with this guy or break up with him. Girls, it is a difficult choice. I know some of you are tired of fighting the yoke. You know what it means to symbolically have your oxygen cut off because you are always trying to move him a direction he does not want to go. Let me encourage you, that you have permission to break up and be free. It will not be easy, but you will feel a lot lighter with the weight of the yoke lifted from your shoulders.

I know letting this guy go is not going to be easy. But let's imagine together what your life may look like if you do not break up or continue to date non-Christians.

Fast forward your life, and now you are 25 years old. You are getting married to a non-Christian. He is hot, funny and nice; everything you wanted, but not a Christian. After you get married your marriage is mediocre at best, and because he does not go to church you do not go either. In the back of your mind you know you should be going to church, but you have ignored that still small voice until it stopped bugging you.

As you continue fast-forwarding a few years, you decide to have a baby, a few of them, actually. As a good

136

mom, you would like to take your children to church. However, your husband is still not saved and certainly not going to church. You get in arguments over whether the family should go to church or not, and then one day you decide you have had enough and are going to church whether he goes or not.

At church, you really feel God's drawing presence and know you need God in your life again. You go to the altar, repent and feel all clean and new inside again. At home, over lunch, you share this rekindled passion for the Lord with your husband and to your dismay he gets upset about you becoming a "goody Christian" on him when he knows the real you. You fight every Sunday about going to church, the kids are divided between mom and dad, and you have to make a decision to follow Jesus or your spouse.

This is a made-up scenario, but I know, and you may too, real people who are living this today. Pray and ask God to give you wisdom and guidance in how to leave this relationship in a positive way. God has ways of giving us words to help us do what He knows is best for us.

Hot Topic #2: Half-virgins

"I have not had sex, therefore I'm a virgin." Recently I was talking to a teenage friend of mine who is 15 years old, and he said in his high school, they have what they call "half-virgins." I was not familiar with the term, but he said guys know which girls are virgins and which ones are easy to sleep with. He said they know who has slept with whom and how many guys a girl has been with.

If that was not shocking enough, he continued, the guys also know who the "half-virgins" are. He explained "half-virgins" were girls who are technically virgins but partake in oral sex or other inappropriate acts with guys. (Side note: I am sorry if I have to use some terms unusual to you. If you do not know what they mean, you can ask your parents, e-mail me or ignore it. I put in these terms because today most teens know this stuff, but if you do not please forgive me.)

The Bible says in Ephesians 5:26-27, "…Just as Christ loved the church and gave himself up for her to make her holy, cleansing her by the washing with water through the Word, and to present her to himself as a radiant church, without stain or wrinkle or any other blemish, but holy and blameless."

Let's go back to our gift illustration. If the gift is half-used is it new? If you can describe yourself as a "half-virgin," are you pure? I want you to be a bride without stain or wrinkle. I want your gift to not look like it has been re-wrapped. Think of what it would be like to re-use wrapping paper. It would be wrinkled and maybe even torn. Used wrapping paper is impossible to smooth and look brand new. I want you to be able to be without stain, wrinkle or blemish on your wedding night.

Psalm 101:3 says, "I will set before my eyes no vile thing."

For some ladies, this half-virgin, half-purity idea may include pornography for you. It can tend to be a guy addiction, but girls can be trapped by it, too. Let us not even give the devil a chance to get his foot in the door. We should be careful to guard what we allow our eyes to see.

Hot Topic #3: Homosexuality

What does the Bible say about homosexuality? Most of your friends have gotten their view of it from what they hear others saying. That is why I want you to see what the Bible says about it. Then you will know firsthand.

The Bible talks about this topic in both the Old and New Testaments. On this subject, contrary to what a lot of people will try to say, the Bible is not silent.

> Leviticus 18:22, "Do not lie with a man as one lies with a woman; that is detestable."

>Romans 1:26, "Because of this, God gave them over to shameful lusts. Even their women exchanged natural relations for unnatural ones."

>I Corinthians 6:9, "Do you not know that the wicked will not inherit the kingdom of God? Do not be deceived: Neither the sexually immoral nor idolaters nor adulterers nor male prostitutes nor homosexual offenders nor thieves nor the greedy nor drunkards nor slanderers nor swindlers will inherit the kingdom of God."

According to the Bible, God does not approve of homosexuality. Just because the world has chosen to accept it does not change the Word of God. God's Word is unchanging and the standard by which we must live our lives.

What if one day we decide that there are too many people committing adultery and instead of making them all stop their sin, we just change our view? Does that make it right? No. Just because some states say prostitution is legal, does not make it legal according to the Bible. As Christians, we have to have a standard by which to live. If not, our nation and world would be in total chaos.

I heard a story once about a little boy who did not want to follow the rules. His parents decided in order to teach him why there were rules, they would imagine together, with their son, what life would be like with no rules. Imagine with them, if you and your family wanted to go to the zoo. When you arrive, the zoo is not open, because the zoo workers decided not to show up for work simply because no one could make them. When you arrive back at your home, there are people living in your home, because no one could make them leave. The mailperson stole your mail, because there were no consequences for stealing. You and your friends never go to school since no one could enforce the rules that kids go to school. Even your bank would not have to give you your money, because there would be no laws to protect your accounts from someone else asking for your money.

Do you see how rules allow our society to function in an orderly fashion? Ladies, it is God Himself who knew we would need order. God gave the first law in the Garden of Eden to the very first man and woman, and to our surprise, they broke the one law they were given to follow and were banned from paradise forever. Later in the book of Exodus,

God gave the Ten Commandments as a guideline for people to coexist.

My husband and I have gone on several mission trips to Haiti, and it is a frustrating experience because just like we are talking about, there is no one to enforce the rules. It is common for people to steal from others without consequences, and adultery is rampant, leaving broken women and abandoned children everywhere. Haiti is an example of a nation who threw out God and the Bible. The society is chaotic as a result. I pray America will follow the Bible, because by doing so we are blessed. By following the Word of God we have great abundance and blessing from our Lord. We need to not allow sinners to twist our beliefs so that sin is tolerated. If the Bible says it is wrong, it is wrong!

These three hot topics: Dating non-Christians, half-virgins and homosexuality are tough areas. If you have a youth group, these may be some topics to discuss with your youth pastor and youth group. We need to be biblically strong on where we stand and memorize the scriptures listed in this chapter so we know why we believe what we believe.

Discussion Questions

1. Is it wrong to date non-Christians? How do you know if a guy is a Christian or not?
2. How far is too far to go with a guy? Where is the line?
3. Can people be born homosexuals or is it a sin?

It Is The Little Things That Matter

~~~~

"Catch for us the foxes, the little foxes that ruin the vineyards."
Song of Solomon 2:15

Record rainfalls saturated South Dakota during the summer of 2010. Every time the meteorologists predicted it was going to rain, we would get 1 to 3 inches. The rainfall totals for the year were off the charts, but we felt grateful our basement did not flood as we knew many people who encountered this misfortune. The only leakage of water that we had was in the track of our sliding glass doors. It would get full of water and overflow into our dining room. Each time it rained I had to be sure I was home to soak up the water with towels. When it rained in the middle of the night, I would get up and change the towels all night long, and it became frustrating.

I had to figure out how to fix this problem. The Internet said to find the weep holes in your door and make sure they were not clogged. I did not know where to start, but I began cleaning gunk from my doors in search of a weep hole. I dug out mud, dog hair and carpet threads from every possible place I could see that was a hole in my door. Suddenly, I saw it. Outside on the very bottom of the door, under a ledge was a little slit. I took a paperclip and jammed it into the slit. Water started to flow out of that hole, and the hole began draining water that had been trapped in our sliding glass door track. I was so happy to be free of this burden.

Why do I tell you such a silly story? It is because in life sometimes it is the little things that matter. The hole in my door did not get jammed by a major catastrophe -- it was not a leaf or a large object that had clogged it. It was one piece of dirt, then another piece and again, another piece. Each of these insignificant pieces of dirt stuck to the next piece and formed a blockage causing flooding to my home and could have caused significant damage if I had not carefully mopped up the water in the track throughout each rain storm.

As I thought about this little, tiny, itsy, bitsy half-inch hole causing such havoc on my life, I thought about our lives. It is not the big things that bring us down. We are smart enough to see the big things and avoid them. It is the little compromises - saying, "I am strong enough to date," "I can be alone with a guy," "I am strong enough to not sleep with him," "I can date non-Christian guys," "He is so hot! How can I say no?" "I can make-out and not do any damage," I can... I can... and the compromises begin to pile up.

"I do not need to go to church every Sunday. Missing one time will not hurt," "I do not need to read my Bible today," "I do not have time to pray this morning," one by one, our lives fill up with junk. At first, we do not always see it. Sometimes, we do not even notice as we feel safe and OK. Everything seems fine when suddenly, something happens, and we realize there is a huge blockage in the way. We cannot even see, feel or touch God, but we wonder how we got so far away from Him.

From now on I will be cleaning out those weep holes in our door regularly. We could have a lot of damage in our home if I ever let that slip, and I think of my spiritual life in the same perspective. I want to keep a short account with God, and when I sin, I want to immediately ask for forgiveness. I want to stay clean through worship and prayer and reading my Bible and not let the junk build up in my life.

Being God's girl is an amazing privilege. He is the King, and I am His princess. So are you. I want to make Him proud by living according to His Word and His principles. He died on the cross for me, and at the very least I can serve Him and encourage you to come along with me! You can make it, sister, from wherever you are now to your wedding night into your happily ever after. Purity is possible! You can make it, you are God's girl!

> You can make it, you are God's girl!

Discussion Questions

1. What are the "little things" in your life that are keeping you from purity?
2. What is the best way to keep a short account with God?
3. Is purity possible in your life?

Endnotes

~~~~

Your Sins Will Find You Out

1. Meador, C. (2002). *Types of STD's*. Retrieved from http://www.essortment.com/all/typesstds_rcjh.htm
2. Weinstock H et al., Sexually transmitted diseases among American youth: incidence and prevalence estimates, 2000, *Perspectives on Sexual and Reproductive Health*, 2004, 36(1):6–10.
3. United Nations Statistics Division. (2006). *Demographic Yearbook 2006*. New York: United Nations.
4. Guttmacher Institute, *U.S. Teenage Pregnancies, Births and Abortions: National and State Trends and Trends by Race and Ethnicity*, accessed Jan. 26, 2010.

Are Drugs For God's Girl?

1. *Drug abuse/sorceries*. (2001, March 12). Retrieved from http://philologos.org/bpr/files/misc_studies/ms079.htm

Biographies of contributing sources

~~~~

Dr. Addison Tolentino, MD, attended medical school at the University of the Philippines College of Medicine in Manila. He did his internal medicine residency at the Montefiore Medical Center, Albert Einstein College of Medicine in Bronx, New York. He was trained in medical oncology and hematology at the Stony Brook University Hospital in Stony Brook, New York, and is Board Certified by the American Board of Internal Medicine in the specialties of Internal Medicine, Medical Oncology and Hematology. He is a medical oncologist and hematologist at the Avera Cancer Institute in Sioux Falls, South Dakota.

Dr. Brian Kidman, MD, is a native of Huron, South Dakota. He completed his medical training and graduated from Texas Tech University School of Medicine in 1985. He then completed his family practice training in 1988 at Sioux Falls Family Practice

Residency Program, now known as Center for Family Medicine in Sioux Falls, South Dakota. Since finishing his residency training, Dr. Kidman has practiced in different medical settings, including at the Sioux Falls Veteran's Hospital, emergency medicine at several hospitals and at Sanford Health in Sioux Falls. He is married to Stephanie and has two daughters, Anna and Katie. He loves to travel, especially to other countries where he has provided much medical mission work over the years.

About The Author

~~~~~

Rachel Johnson is an ordained Assembly of God minister. She graduated from North Central Bible College in 1996. She and her husband, Jeremiah, were worship and youth pastors in Susanville, California, for four years and now serve as worship and young adult pastors at First Assembly of God in Sioux Falls, South Dakota.

Rachel has been married to Jeremiah Johnson for more than 10 years and they have two daughters, Zoe and Gabrielle. Rachel has also authored *Gabrielle's Journey*, a true story of her and Jeremiah's youngest daughter born 10 weeks premature on Christmas break, 24 hours from home.

Rachel is a wife, mom, worship leader, author and speaker. Rachel would love to come speak at your church or youth group.

Contact Information

~~~~

Jeremiah and Rachel Johnson
6300 West 41st Street
Sioux Falls, South Dakota 57106
(605) 413-3875
jerandrach@hotmail.com